THE GARDENS OF IRELAND
A Visitor's Guide

A Paperback Original
First published 1990 by
Poolbeg Press Ltd
Knocksedan House,
Swords, Co Dublin, Ireland

© Jack Whaley, 1990

ISBN 1 85371 073 3

These pieces were originally published in *The Irish Times*

Editor: Steve Waldren
Cover photograph of Powerscourt Gardens, Enniskerry, Co Wicklow
Cover design and photography by Maria Walshe
Set by Richard Parfrey in Times 11 pt.
Printed by the Guernsey Press Ltd
Vale, Guernsey, Channel Islands

THE GARDENS OF IRELAND
A Visitor's Guide

POOLBEG

Jack Whaley

Acknowledgements

The author, the editor, Steve Waldren, and the publishers would like to express their gratitude for information and help given by the owners, proprietors, directors or management of the gardens discussed in this book.

Contents

Introduction

The gardens of Ireland are almost as variable as the climate, which seldom repeats itself for more than two days in succession. Many may contain a similar plant range but with a very different setting. Gardens in some of the European continental countries and in Britain often possess more grandeur, having being created by professional designers who indulged the exotic fancies of their employers, with the construction of lavish embellishments such as artificial watercourses featuring spectacular fountains, and statuary executed by the leading exponents of the art. The fact that no such elaborate masterpieces ever existed in Ireland may be ascribed to the non-existence here of industrial barons and noble families, who often were in competition to build magnificent palaces with gardens to match or complement their stately splendour.

Instead of the ducal estates to be found in Britain and on the continent, the Irish versions were modest in size and opulence. In fact many owners lived in very impecunious circumstances, and while the majority showed little interest in gardening, those that did gave considerable dedication to their pursuit. Unable to afford the services of leading landscape designers, most of the design work sprang from the personal inspirations of the owners. As a consequence gardens of marked originality emerged. Sometimes a mingling of French and English styles can be detected in the composition of many of the country's leading gardens. These are however just small auxiliary features. In general it may be said that Irish gardens have been constructed around natural features such as rivers, streams, cliff heights and other indigenous features. This is a complete reversal of the process used to create the great gardens of Europe.

In Ireland the number of privately owned and sometimes maintained gardens is still large and includes such famous and illustrious gardens as Birr Castle, Mount Usher, Fernhill and Annes Grove. There are others, but these four embody some of the finest examples of Irish gardening. Mount Usher provides an example of a garden designed, built and planted by a family with outstanding engineering and botanical talents.

Those Irish gardens now under state control are receiving dedicated care from their new administrators and, since the time interval has been short, still retain some of the former atmosphere of private ownership. That delectable island set in the azure blue waters offshore Cork, called Garinish, is a perfect example of simple individuality and possibly has the most individual appeal of the public sector gardens.

The detailed description of all the gardens included in this book will provide the plant enthusiast with information on where many rare and interesting plants may be seen. All would fall into the category of shrub gardens, though some contain limited herbaceous plantings. With the exception of Powerscourt, informality is very much the keynote. The symmetrical design of the Victorian gardening era apparently did not penetrate to Ireland and no large-scale examples of this gardening fashion are to be found. One other factor which has a very significant bearing on the plant-growing potential in Ireland is its geographical position. Not alone have great benefits been derived from the fact that the country lies in the direct path of the Gulf Stream, but with nothing to the west except thousands of miles of ocean, whence come the prevailing winds, the pollution problem which today threatens much of Europe is almost totally absent.

Altamont

County Carlow

Altamont Gardens, Ballon, Co Carlow
Telephone: Not Listed

Take the main road south from Dublin for 50 miles (81 Km) as far as Tullow. Continue along the road from Tullow to Bunclody for 4 miles (6.5 Km), then turn left to follow the signpost for the gardens.

This is a garden which spreads itself over a widely different terrain beginning with a semblance of formality and ending in an ice age ravine screened with primeval oak forest into which have recently been introduced some very exotic rhododendrons.

The feature which most nearly approaches the concept of a formal garden is the view of the 2.5 acre lake set in a direct line from the house to which it is linked by an equally direct Broad Walk running straight to the water's edge. This walk is set with formal boxwood edgings and is spanned at its middle distance by a "castellated golden yew arch attended by spirally clipped individual yews" two of which are golden. During the dredging of the lake one of these was trodden upon by an earth excavator and was replaced by a 30-year-old substitute taken from another part of the garden. While other trees might provide problems in re-establishment, a yew of this age is still in its childhood.

The gardens are entered by the Nun's Walk whose historical origins date back to the 17th century. Along this right hand boundary running parallel to the Broad Walk stretches a magnificent line of mature beech trees probably planted around 200 years ago. Beautiful in their spring dressing of soft green, they also provide an autumn colour display difficult to equal.

Continuing along the walk towards the house, which dates back to the mid seventeenth century, a blending of small growing or dwarf plants fills a large rectangular bed. In spring a collection of specially selected elite daffodils and species tulips add a colourful touch among the wide ranging collection of dwarf conifers. Contained in this border are several unusual and in some cases rare plants. *Daphne odora*, a fragrant early flowering, rather tender Chinese species, is very seldom seen and is grown in few other Irish gardens. The always admired *Abies koreana* is seen as a young plant already carrying its beautiful purple-blue cones. Spruce listed here as *Picea koreana*, the seed of which was obtained from the Peking Botanical Gardens, might well be *Picea koyamae* which originally bore the name *Picea koraiensis*. This tree is said to be restricted to one small grove growing at 5-6,000 feet in Central Japan, although it occurs rather more frequently in Korea.

This bed also contains a number of dwarf rhododendrons which include the slender growing *R.* "Yellow Hammer" with yellow bell shaped flowers, and the shapely *R. yakushimanum* showing shades of variable pink and white according to the age of the corolla. In the shelter of the house a magnificent *Rhododendron augustinii* rises to 30 feet. Presiding over this border is a stately specimen of *Abies procera*, below which grows a spreading bush of that excellent subject for autumn colouring, *Parrotia persica*, and nearby a miniature *Abies procera* "Nana".

The Broad Walk which calls invitingly for a stroll down to the lakeside is bordered by beds of florabunda and old shrub roses. These change to a collection of species and old fashioned roses along the spur walk following the right hand side of the lake. Before embarking on this trail there are a profusion of good plants to admire. The *Cedrus deodara* claims to be all of 140 years, planted around the time the lake itself was dug out to provide employment during the Famine years. Further back a large well furnished fern-leaved beech is rather too clustered to reveal its full beauty or form. Closer to the lake a 30-year-old *Davidia* provides a decorative picture when festooned with its handkerchief like bracts. A similarly aged tulip tree flowers regularly, despite storm damage to its top.

It is only to be expected that this lake should lend itself to the introduction of moisture-loving plants. Two such genera are much in evidence. Firstly the swamp cypresses are represented by the more usual *Taxodium distichum* and the lesser known *Taxodium ascendens,* so attractive in early summer with its beady buds and later in autumn when its colour can be spectacular. Here too some strongly growing specimens of *Metasequoia glyptostroboides*, related to *Taxodium,* are enjoying the moist soil conditions. This garden contains a large number of acers, including *A. ginnala,* many growing around the lakeside. In addition a pleasing planting of a birch in an overhanging position mirrors itself in the water. Looking down the lake towards the island at the upper end there can be seen an old *Rhododendron arboreum* raised from seed by the father of the present owner. It is the only survivor of many seedlings of this species which succumbed to the severe frost of 1980. The colour of this plant is a soft rose pink.

Rhododendrons are well represented and widely dispersed throughout the gardens, perhaps by a deliberate consciousness that the massing of this outstanding genus only detracts from their individual charms. I noticed that splendid hybrid of *R. campylocarpum*, the white flowering pink-tinged *R.* "Unique", and a well developed specimen of *R. cinnabarinum*. This is the type plant, not the plum shaded var. *roylei* which is slightly more tender, and in these parts might require a wall.

This last mentioned rhododendron is growing at the end of a border of *Paeonia,* of which this garden boasts a fairly large collection. Further along the old croquet ground an azalea collection serves the dual purpose of providing a wide range of colour in early summer and an equal diversity of autumn tints.

Over the bridge which spans the feeder end of the lake lies an area of newly developed garden. Here a collection of assorted plants have been assembled which include *Acer, Viburnum, Cornus* and a very showy *Exochorda* X *macrantha* "The Bride", its drooping branches smothered with racemes of pure white flowers.

Returning by the path behind the lake, a medium sized *Sequoiadendron giganteum* catches the attention. It is festooned with ivy providing good winter shelter for some of the birds, including a few rarities, with which this garden abounds. In a parkland field across the boundary stands another *Sequoiadendron giganteum* in complete isolation apart from one neighbouring oak *Quercus robur* "Concordia". The redwood tree is said to have been planted to commemorate the battle of Waterloo, albeit some years after this decisive battle had been fought, since the earliest introduction of this Californian tree was in 1853. Further along a 30-year-old *Tsuga heterophylla* makes a graceful and imaginative piece of planting. In this same area a large *Cornus kousa* provides a spectacle of unrivalled beauty during June when covered in its pink-tinged bracts.

Nearing the end of the lake, where an enclosing low wall is a further piece of famine relief work, are two *Quercus ilex* of some botanical interest. These trees, whose branches hang over the water, have heavily indented leaves some 5 inches long and 2.5 inches in width, double the size of the *Q. ilex* type. These trees might appear to be the *Q. ilex* cultivar "Genabii" but there have arisen many variations from the type, since *Q. ilex* is very polmorphic in character.

The stream falling away from the lake level can be followed throughout its descent to the low valley of the Slaney river. The planting of a ribbon arboretum following the line of this watercourse is continuing, with the earlier plantings having already reached some size. One, a *Drimys winteri* of 15 years carried its first flowers in the fourteenth year, a useful guideline for those who, having planted this very showy white-flowered tree-sized shrub, are wondering when they will be rewarded with a flower. *Embothrium* are growing fast in the moisture of this glade providing a dazzling display of vivid scarlet flowers. The snow gum *Eucalyptus niphophila*, not regarded as being among the hardiest of the genus, is here making excellent growth. A rather special *Syringa* deserves a mention. This is *S.* X *josiflexa* "Bellicent", distinguished by its very large panicles of rose pink flowers. The plant has Canadian origins.

The stream now drops rapidly through what are almost certainly remnants of the original indigenous oak woods which some thousands of years ago covered most of the country. As is usual in this type of woodland, the trees, trying to eke out an existence on very poor rocky soil, are distorted in their growth and provide a very arresting view of their branch tracery. Here and there where pockets of richer soil exists one or two good *Rhododendron* species have been introduced. Among those I noticed were the April-flowering *R. rex* carrying large tight trusses of white pink-tinged flowers with a basal crimson stain. Close by is a planting of *R. calophytum* which must rank among the finest and easiest to grow of the large leaved types. Its trusses are rather looser than *R. rex* and reveal more pink, but the leaves are impressive being all of 7 inches long and oblong lanceolate in shape.

Along the lower reaches of this chasm may be seen a most interesting rock formation said by geologists to have been formed during the ice age. The rocks subjected to the massive pressures exerted by the ice show very marked fissures. At the bottom of the valley the river Slaney offers splendid fishing prospects.

Annes Grove

County Cork

Annes Grove, Castletownroche, Co Cork
Telephone: 022 / 26145

Castletownroche is situated half-way between Mallow and Fermoy on the Killarney/Fermoy road. The gardens are 1.5 miles (2.5 Km) north of the town.

The Awbeg river is instrumental in providing moisture essential to the growth of the many waterside plants that flourish in and enhance this outstanding garden.

Annes Grove, the third major garden in County Cork, unlike its two companions Fota and Garinish, is situated well inland, one mile north of Castletownroche. Nonetheless it enjoys a specially favoured microclimate all of its own. Thirty acres of garden maintained in immaculate condition by its dedicated young owner, Mr Annesley, provide a variety of plant life that ensures the display is maintained over a long period if not indeed on a muted scale throughout the entire year.

Water must be an important factor in creating this plant-favouring microclimate because, like the other great inland garden at Birr Castle, Annes Grove is served by a river. The Awbeg dawdles through the entire length of the garden, falling over tiny weirs and providing the essential moisture required by the many waterside plants which clothe its banks. Trees have been sited in such a way that views of the river are frequent from different vantage points.

The architecture of Annes Grove House reveals its 18th-century origins with the walled garden of the same period properly hidden out of sight. The parkland profile which no doubt prevailed has been gradually altered by period plantings. In front of the house a thin semi-circular avenue of lime trees may still be detected. Good specimen trees of Victorian age adorn the drive. The garden entered the modern age around the start of the century when the present owner's grandfather, as a contributor to the plant-collecting expeditions, obtained many of the plants which enrich this garden today.

The deep shade of the Victorian driveway plantings limit the additions that can be introduced here. There are, however, some fine original trees including the Californian *Abies magnifica*, 66 feet in height and the more showy Japanese *Picea jezoensis* with its young scarlet cones. In 1968 this was recorded as measuring 50 feet.

Close to the house a grove of evergreen oaks *Quercus ilex*, includes the rare, large-leaved variety "Bicton", which originated in Devon. The sheltered stable yard behind the house contains varieties of the Californian *Ceanothus*, the European *Colutea arborescens* with its conspicuous pea-like flowers, and the more tender *Feijoa sellowiana*, shy to flower in this protected but shady position. In front of the house a tulip tree, approaching flowering age, has for neighbours two good cedars, *Cedrus atlantica* and *C. atlantica* forma *glauca*, the blue form.

So on to the walled garden fancifully laid out with a small *parterre*, box edged and filled with bedding plants. On the rise above an attractive garden house, formerly with a brush-wood thatch but now conventionally roofed in blending tiles, is a good dark form of *Cryptomeria japonica* "Elegans", a tree whose copper tinted foliage is developed during the winter months. To the rear of the summer house a plant of *Camellia reticulata*, the tender Chinese species with its rose pink trumpet-shaped flowers set off with golden stamens, is a splendid sight. A small pond overhung with a drooping birch adds to the idyllic charm of this secluded garden.

Other furnishings include the New Zealand *Pseuodopanax crassifolius*, killed in many Irish gardens in the winter of 1978, and a very well-developed bush of *Eucryphia* X *nymansensis* "Nymansay". The walls, both inside and out-side, provide space for some of the more tender climbers and wall shrubs. Several young *Cestrum* "Newellii" may be seen displaying their ruby-red trumpet flowers in late May, just outside the gateway.

The approach to the less formal sections of the garden is gradual. The path towards the river valley is flanked on one side by a grass lawn set with specimen elms, two of which have, unfortunately, succumbed to the deadly Dutch elm disease causing removal problems, while on the other side an extensive shrub border contains a very large *Gleditsia triacanthos* featured by frond-like leaves and long, brown pods. The border culminates in a panoramic view of the river, tumultuous in its colour range at most seasons, provided by the hillside shrubs and trees, the broken water of the river blended with the richness of the waterside flora. This, in essence, is Annes Grove, a creation dating from the first World War when convalescent troops from Fermoy assisted in its construction.

The broad walk continues left through the main upland shrub plantings. On the left, well protected, probably unnecessarily, is a fine *Drimys lanceolata* with small copper-tinted leaves, aromatic when bruised, and tiny white flowers. This is not as spectacular a plant as *D. winteri* but perhaps more refined. June, when flowering begins to wane, will still see *Cornus kousa* var. *chinensis* at its very best covered with white rose-tinted bracts. The earlier May-flowering *C. nuttallii* further along is also good but decidedly more tender. Its bracts are also white but in addition it can provide brilliant autumn red and yellow colouring. *Myrtus apiculata*, which seems to crop up in all Irish gardens, is also here displaying its two-tone bark.

But by far the most prevalent plants in this garden are the *Hoheria* which are seeding themselves with complete abandon and possibly hybridising into the bargain. Young plants of this genus can be very difficult if not impossible to identify with their ever-changing leaf size and formation. A bush of *Pieris taiwanensis* gives a pleasing albeit a more subdued effect than the flamboyant *P. formosa* var. *forrestii*. This is an excellent colour shrub in early June, which also has attractive long racemes of flowers not unlike those of lily of the valley.

Next come the rhododendrons, and what a very wide

ranging collection has been assembled here. Not all are labelled, and since many are derived from seed sent home by Kingdon Ward and other plant collectors, some very interesting plants may be found as identification proceeds. This work is still in progress and when completed a proper catalogue of all the plants is envisaged.

There is a fine plant of *R.* "Cornubia", a deep red obtained by crossing *R. arboreum* with *R.* "Shilsonii", but hardly an improvement on the latter parent and decidedly more tender. *R. delavayi*, another of the *arboreum* series, is developing into tree size carrying its compact trusses of blood red blooms in late March or April and, like its neighbour, is equally tender and only suited to favoured localities. Further along on a side spur there is a planting of blues, including "Blue Tit" and "Blue Diamond" which possess a common parent in the illustrious *R. augustinii*. On the opposite side of the walk a collection of young *Camellia* promises well.

Lower down the hillside the stately *R. falconeri* shows off its large dome shaped creamy yellow flowers. The rather delicate *Magnolia* X *watsonii* looking very healthy here must offer a strong appeal with the fragrance of the large saucer shaped white flowers set with crimson anthers.

The path descending towards the river leads through further plantings of rhododendrons interspersed with conifers. A very good *Juniperus recurva* var. *coxii* lends a note of elegance with its weeping slender branches. Nearby a large bush of *Rhododendron wardii*, named after Kingdon Ward, adds its yellow lustre. The *R. cinnabarinum* group is well represented with the variety *blandfordiiflorum* outstanding. This form has its tubular flowers red on the outside and yellow inside.

One of several *Metasequoia* has made good growth enjoying conditions in this moist valley. A small tree of *Camellia saluenensis* covers itself in flowers of delicate pink. But for rich colour nothing can surpass the brilliant crimson of *Embothrium coccineum*. An *Azara microphylla* has climbed to a commanding height of 30 feet scenting the surrounding air. A neighbouring thorn *Crataegus arnoldiana* bears remarkable cherry sized scarlet fruits.

Less obtrusive but nevertheless of passing interest are the group of *Cassinia leptophylla*. This New Zealand foliage shrub, generally hardy, has small greyish leaves with yellow under surfaces and white flower heads appearing in August. Two southern hemisphere conifers present a tropical effect. The Chilean *Podocarpus salignus* has reached tree size, but its New Zealand counterpart *P. totara* has proved itself a slower grower.

Down beside the river all sorts of water plants abound enjoying the moisture laden soil beside the slow moving stream criss-crossed by rustic bridges. A large island of *Primula florindae* has flowers of sulphur yellow carried on long 30 inch stems. Colonies of *Lysichiton* live along the water edge displaying their yellow spathes in late spring while shades of pink are provided by the umbrella plant, *Peltiphyllum peltatum*. Scattered clumps of bamboos assist in creating an exotic effect aided by the architectural *Gunnera manicata*.

This as a garden is still developing, having an owner with a desire to expand and improve and meeting with obvious success. It is to be hoped that his attempts to introduce new plants from seed collected in Crete will bear fruit, but the contrast between this highly humid valley and the rainless and extremely hot summers of Crete must result in some disappointments. But even limited success would be a great achievement and it is an encouraging factor that already some Mediterranean plants such as *Cistus parviflorus* and *Helianthemum appeninum* have been long established here.

Ashbourne House Hotel

County Cork

Ashbourne House Hotel, Glounthane, Co Cork
Telephone: 021 / 353319

Situated in Glounthane, 6 miles (10 Km) east of Cork on the road to Youghal.

This is a garden which probably is not very widely known. Those who have discovered it will be aware that it is a garden of considerable distinction, those who have yet to do so have a very great pleasure in store. Its original owner, Richard Beamish Henrik, 1862-1888, had close connections with Kew, and this garden profited largely from these associations. The archives at Kew bear record of the many plants which were sent from Kew to the owners of Ashbourne House. Not all, but a very sizeable proportion of these are still alive. The fact that Ashbourne House has now become a hotel has in no way diminished its garden appeal. The gardens are still being maintained in reasonably good order by an enthusiastic gardener appreciative of her charge.

On the lawn in front of the hotel stands a remarkable *Gymnocladus dioica*, impressive by any standards. This tree, a female with eight-inch-long panicles of greenish-white flowers, is one of the Kew originals. It measures 46 x 4.5 feet, just one foot shorter than the specimen to be seen at Kew itself. Known as the Kentucky coffee tree in America, its beans were roasted as a coffee substitute. Its bipinnate leaves are up to three feet long and two feet wide. The skeleton leaf stalks remain on the tree for some time after the leaf tissue branchlets have fallen.

In the woodland behind, the Chinese *Styrax hemsleyana* makes a charming sight in June when hung with racemes of pure white flowers from which protrude its golden yellow anthers. This shade-loving tree does not take so kindly to open positions but is hardy anywhere. Near the entrance gate a stream or wet ditch provides a suitable home for the colourful yellow *Lysichiton americanus* and other aquatic plants. A bed of candelabra *Primula* has recently been introduced and will continue to form a most attractive feature of the garden.

Towards the back of the hotel the flamboyant rich red of a massed group of *Cestrum elegans* provide a magnetic attraction during their long flowering period. This South American charmer is the envy of most inland gardeners in northern regions, who find spring frosts eventually prove fatal. In this middle area the main *Rhododendron* are to be found. Most of these are hybrids tending towards the azalea types which provide subtle pastel colourings. This is not in any sense a *Rhododendron* garden, but rather a wide collection of plants which include many good representatives of the genus.

Nothing here is perhaps more spectacular than *Magnolia campbellii* and a source of much local pride. This tree measures around 50 feet with a proportionate spread which, when covered in spring with several hundred pink blossoms, is a truly memorable sight. Incidentally, the first recording flowering of *M. campbellii* in the British Isles was at Lakelands in Co Cork.

Conifers are represented by several very good specimens. These include three large *Ginkgo biloba*, the tallest of which when last measured was 59 feet and one of the largest in Ireland. At that time there was also recorded a very large *Cedrus deodara*, unfortunately since uprooted, its trunk still lying where it fell. Today there still remains a very large *Cedrus atlantica* forma *glauca* in excellent health. Southern hemisphere conifers are represented by the Chilean *Podocarpus andinus* and the always picturesque *Pinus armandii*, its clusters of huge banana shaped cones framed in its glaucous foliage. A planting date for this tree has been given as 1914.

The yew hedges and arches in the lower part of the garden, planted many decades ago and carefully tended by many gardeners, are still intact conveying a sense of the garden's antiquity. At a junction along this yew path a *Pseudopanax arboreus* forms a spreading shrub rather than a tree. Its large flower clusters later give way to black fruits. There is a specimen of this tree in Fota Island garden which was obtained from Ashbourne House in 1948. It might seem that with a garden so famous as Fota on its doorstep traffic in plants towards Ashbourne House might have occurred, but there is no evidence to show that such movement ever took place.

There are few problems in growing *Eucalyptus* in this part of the country so it might be assumed that some of the most tender species would be found growing here, as indeed they do. The silver gum *E. cordata*, regarded by many as the most decorative of all the eucalypts, has made an outstanding specimen. It seems surprising that this species coming from south Tasmania should be less than hardy, but so it has proved in all but the most favoured gardens.

Claims could be laid that the most spectacular event in any garden is the flowering of the embothriums. Here in these southern areas this plant reaches a colour perfection seldom seen elsewhere and a visit to this garden in early June will find *E. coccineum* var. *longifolium* displaying its mantle of crimson-scarlet tubular racemes. This tree also produces a beautifully grained timber but seldom attains any great size. It also provides excellent firewood.

Along the boundary walk behind the tennis courts a large *Colletia cruciata* makes an impressive showing not so much with its white flowers appearing in late summer and autumn, but by its formidable display of sharp pointed flat triangular shaped fleshy leaves. The appearance of this plant suggests it might belong to a xeric type terrain but in fact it comes from Uruguay, certainly not the driest of countries. The viburnums, represented here by *V. plicatum* "Mariesii," can hold their own in any plant company, and this when seen in full flower with its layers of snowbell-like flowers is a real gem.

Ashbourne House, whose limited size forbids its ever ranking as a major Irish garden, is nevertheless of considerable historical importance in both the quality and derivation of its plants, not to mention its attractions for less scientifically minded gardeners who will greatly enjoy the beauty of its considerable range of trees and shrubs.

Fota Island

County Cork

Fota, Cobh, Co Cork
Telephone: 021 / 812678

From Cork, take the road to Youghal for 7 miles (11 Km). Turn right on to the road for Cobh and follow signposts for Fota.

This historical garden, tracing its origins from the late 18th century, is now under the administration of University College Cork. Fota House is also open to the public. The University purchased the estate in 1975, from which date began the planning which has resulted in its present development and renovation after a period of neglect. Situated in Cork harbour only eight miles from the city centre, excellent communications are provided by the railway link between Cork and Waterford which passes through Fota, where by special arrangement with its previous owner all trains are compelled to halt.

Adjacent and complementary to the garden a Wildlife Park comprising 70 acres under the patronage of the Dublin Zoological Society provides a more diversified appeal to those in search of a natural environment. Visitors can transverse the open areas allotted to the more dangerous animals by means of a road train.

The gardens must always remain the topmost attraction in this complex with their collection of over 1,000 trees and shrubs, many of which are now of historical importance, being numbered among the first plantings of certain species in the British Isles. The original owners of Fota, the Smith-Barry family and their ancestors, commenced the building of these gardens around 1820 and some of the older trees still standing can be dated from this period. They had an ambition to create a garden here to rank with the best in Britain and went well on the way to succeeding. It is important to record that this family were not merely dilettante gardeners, but plantsmen of a very high order who kept detailed records of their plantings, listing the origins of all plants and their growth rates. These records are now carefully treasured by the present owners. History, whether it concerns people or plants, always fascinates and a plant whose history is known creates considerably more interest than one with none. Less fortunately a period of neglect caused the death or the malaise of several very valuable shrubs. Visitors are now privileged to view this garden restored to its former glory. Despite the outside diversions nothing has been altered within the garden and house area to change the atmosphere of this old world garden, whose history stretches back nearly two centuries.

The gardens are entered by a small gateway opposite the car park. If the western perimeter is followed leading towards the house some of the outstanding trees in this collection will be encountered. The sight of the New Zealand *Phyllocladus trichomanoides* planted in 1941, and now attaining a height of 22 feet, the highest in the British Isles, at once reveals the quality of this garden. Other conifers in this area are the ever graceful *Picea breweriana* and a much older *Picea spinulosa* planted in 1914. These weeping spruces are quite magnificent. *Caesalpinia japonica* with its bright yellow flowers and scarlet stamens is both rare and beautiful. A *Drimys winteri* is of historical interest since it is thought to have originated from the seed collected by H.J. Elwes in the Andes during 1901-2. This area also contains those two outstanding Australian shrubs, *Hakea saligna* and *Grevillea rosmarinifolia*, both very tender subjects. The Chinese *Chionanthus retusus*, a smaller version of the American fringe tree, is preferred here.

It is unfortunate that no planting date exists for the conifer *Abies bornmuelleriana*. This very interesting tree is a native of Asia Minor and possesses similarities to *A. cephalonica* and *A. nordmanniana*. The Fota handbook suggests it may be a hybrid between the two, modern taxonomists often consider it a subspecies of the latter. No conifers have so caught the imagination as the genus *Dacrydium* present here in two of its species, *D. cupressinum* with tail-like pendulous branches and *D. franklinii*, planted in 1854, which is among the finest plants on view and at 28 feet is the highest recorded specimen in the British Isles.

A garden of this standing is somewhat naturally not without a *Catalpa* and here the one chosen is *C. ovata*, the Chinese species, which outgrows most of its relations. The fifty year old *Lomatia ferruginea* has reached a massive size and in late summer presents a spectacular sight when laden with its brown and scarlet flowers. Two more of the many trees which distinguish this garden are the rare but unobtrusive *Liriodendron chinense* and its American counterpart *L. tulipifera* which in 1903 measured 87 feet and is without rival. Another veteran, *Cryptomeria japonica* planted in 1852 just ten years after its first introduction, reached 56 feet in 1892, and is now a massive shapely specimen. A special mention must be accorded to *Freylinia lanceolata* introduced from South Africa in 1774 when it became a popular greenhouse plant but is largely forgotten in modern times which have seen the disappearance of heated greenhouses. The flowers are a restrained creamy white sometimes tipped with pink.

The house, occupying a central position in the gardens, is a comfortable period building of pleasing outline. It, like its surrounds, has been given a new purpose as a developing art gallery and conference centre. Its walls are draped with the blue passion flower, *Passiflora caerulea*, making it blend pleasantly into its surroundings. Towards its parkland frontage more planted areas encircle the house. Here some of the *Eucalyptus* collection numbering at least fifteen species draw admiration. Rare species limited in cultivation include *E. stellulata* from New South Wales and Victoria, which does not reach more than moderate size, and the larger growing *E. viminalis* from Tasmania, which is marked by its tendency to shed its bark in long ribbons, and by its narrow lanceolate leaves.

On the other side of the house a majestic shapely Lebanon cedar planted in 1825 stands opposite the entrance to the walled gardens. The first of these gardens has a vast centre area of well tended lawns. Under the protection of the wall facing the entrance there flourishes a magnificent *Magnolia grandiflora* "Goliath". The other walls provide more than suitable accommodation for some of the more tender plants. These include the very showy Brazilian *Feijoa sellowiana* with edible berries, and crimson-red and white petals with long crimson stamens; the Chinese *Firmiana simplex* whose small yellow panicles of flowers are perhaps secondary to its rich maple-like foliage, and the spectacular *Colquhounia coccinea* var. *mollis*, giving an autumn display of orange scarlet flowers. This area of the garden also contains the *Erica* collections which combine both tree and dwarf types and include the very tender South African *E. pageana* with rich yellow flowers. This is just one of those plants which separates this garden from all others.

The border running along the outside of the walled garden features the very handsome but tender camphor tree, *Cinnamomum camphora*, which provides the camphor of commerce. The Chilean *Myrtus lechleriana* makes a largish bush and flowers freely with the added advantage of being perhaps the hardiest of this genus. A large *Fuchsia* collection makes a colourful display and includes the New Zealand species *F. excorticata* which arrived here from Tresco in 1916.

Further along another historical feature in the shape of the Orangery recalls a period in bygone days when citrus fruits were accorded preferential treatment under heated conditions, their growing being elevated to a status symbol. The presence here of the Kenyan pencil cedar, *Juniperus procera*, planted in 1918 and now 40 feet tall reveals the exceptionally favoured climate prevailing along this southern seaboard. Nowhere else in the country will this tree survive out of doors. Both this and *Juniperus bermudiana* are the largest of their kind in Britain. The unsatisfactory *Abies delavayi* var. *faxoniana* planted in 1916 has succeeded well here albeit not reaching the size of the Powerscourt specimen.

Acer enthusiasts may find the collection here unexciting although including the very lovely *A. triflorum* whose trifoliate leaves colour such a brilliant scarlet. No protection is needed or given to the azaras which are represented by the graceful *A. lanceolata*, a mass of drooping thin leaved greenery and the silvery dome of *A. microphylla* "Variegata".

The depth of some of the genus collections in what was until comparatively recent times a private garden is indeed impressive. At least fifteen *Magnolia* species are on view. These include *M. campbellii* planted here in 1872 just two years after its first introduction to Britain. There can be few plant enthusiasts who would not wish to be able to view this magnificent shrub tree. Besides the species there also figure a number of some of the outstanding hybrids. The camellias have a similar range of representation. No fewer than ten *japonica* hybrids present their varied charms of which few exceed those of the rose-red flowered "Arajishi" with its distinctive toothed tapering leaves, while the shy "Lady Clare" will also have her admirers. This already large collection was further augmented in 1961 by a large group of hybrids sent to Fota from Companhia Horticolo-Agricola Portueme, Porto, Portugal. Another group, the callistemons, arrived rather later, the first planting recorded being that of *C. linearis* in 1941. Now, however, at least eight species are growing successfully in this favoured location.

Two conifers deserve attention in this area. *Pinus armandii* with its attractive clusters of large cones has since its planting in 1917 reached the record height of 61 feet. The other, *Pinus pinea*, may be quite a commonplace tree but not so many owners can lay claim to a tree planted in 1847.

As yet the rhododendrons in which the garden abounds have received no mention but since many of them are to be found around this eastern perimeter of the garden the time is now right to consider what is on view. The flowering period covers almost nine months of the year so that no visit can take in the entire collection. The species include the tree sized *R. arboreum*, the large leaved *R. macabeanum* and *R. falconeri* and the choice *R. crassum*, a sweetly scented late flowering species with pink or white funnel shaped flowers, but a plant that will only survive under very favourable conditions. The very beautiful blue *R. augustinii* var. *chasmanthum* also compels a mention as there is possibly no more attractive rhododendron than this lavender blue beauty. The variety on show here is later than the type and carries larger trusses. The hybrids are also well represented and include some very good *griersonianum* crosses. The soft hunting pink of "Tally Ho" (*griersonianum* X *eriogynum*) and the white-flushed rose of "Amaura" (*griersonianum* X "Penjerrick") are two of very great merit.

Mingling with these exotic colours are some more sombre trees vested with an architectural beauty and of some considerable age. The very long established *Eriobotrya japonica*, first introduced in 1787 and planted here in 1847, has leaves fifteen inches long. If you would like to see rubber present in a tree growing in the British Isles this is provided by *Eucommia ulmoides* which if its leaves are very gently parted will reveal the thin threads of rubber. In this grouping can also be included the New Zealand *Hymenanthera obovata* with very leathery obovate leaves.

Few Australian shrubs are more showy than the *Leptospermum*, of which no fewer than seven varieties can be seen here. The individual flowers may be of no great consequence but massed as these shrubs habitually carry them nothing is more striking than a view of *L. scoparium* "Red Damask" clothed in a red cloak. Unfortunately these are among the most tender of Australian plants. The rare Australian waratah *Telopea truncata*, with individual flowers of very great quality and of a deep crimson colour, makes a spectacular sight.

Despite the rich beauty of these flowering shrubs this garden does not permit one to ignore its trees for very long. At every turn a new antique giant is revealed. A *Torreya californica* was planted here in 1852 and now is seen as a 35-foot high mass of shining green foliage, its long leaves completely covering all its branches. New trees are still being added, none more striking than *Pinus canariensis* which has glaucous leaves when young, although this is lost on mature trees. The specimen here was planted in 1978. Lastly but perhaps the most interesting of all the conifers, the sequoias are represented by a *Sequoia sempervirens* planted, according to the record book, in 1847, exactly one year after the first seed of this North American tree reached Kew; hence this tree, now 102 feet high, must be one of the very first plantings in the British Isles. A slightly taller *Sequoiadendron giganteum* planted in 1854 is but one of many planted around the country on large estate lawns around this time.

It now only remains to take a look at the island, quite small but none the less an island, with all the charm associated with a garden surrounded by water. This island is of recent development, much of its plantings date from 1978. This is a good site for *Salix babylonica* "Aurea", much used as a waterside plant, where its weeping habit and golden appearance can be show to perfection. The white barked *Betula jacquemontii* is another spectacular occupant which will improve with maturity. *Nothofagus dombeyi* also appears here. This Chilean "beech" is partly evergreen, moderately hardy and always decorative. In company with this advance guard a number of rhododendrons have been introduced. These include the dainty rose and white *R. ciliatum*, the deciduous *R. lepidostylum*, a pale yellow rock garden plant, and the variable *R.* "Augfast" with a character similar to its parent *R. augustinii*. Given time this island will become one of the jewels of this magnificent garden.

Garinish Island
(Ilnacullin)

County Cork

Garinish Island, Glengarriff, Co Cork
Telephone: 021 / 63116

From Cork take the road for Bandon (19 miles, 31 Km) to
Bandon. From there follow signposts for Bantry. Garinish is
situated in Glengarriff harbour 11 miles (18 Km) north of
Bantry. Boats are available from Glengarriff Pier. Glengarriff
can also be reached via the mountain road fron Kenmare and
Killarney.

Garinish is an island of 37 acres lying in the sheltered corner of Bantry Bay near Glengariff, enjoying the benefit of the Gulf Stream which gives it a climate exceptionally favourable to plant development. In this respect it has few equals. Only a handful of gardens in these islands enjoy similar conditions.

Never an inhabited island, Garinish first came into prominence when selected by the War Office in the very early nineteenth century as a defence point against the threatened Napoleonic invasions. The Martello tower built then and garrisoned by resident troops may still be seen intact, although the barracks alongside it has long been demolished. This tower now forms a focal point of the gardens.

A century later, when all threats of war had passed, Garinish was sold by the War Office to Scottish MP Annan Bryce, who had realised its gardening potential. He engaged Harold Peto, architect and landscaper, to design a house and garden on Garinish. Peto's design shows Italian Renaissance influence on an otherwise British style. The mansion was never built. The Bryce family maintained and planted the garden with many rare plants until the death of the then owner in 1953, after which it passed into the ownership of the Irish Board of Works. They have continued the planting and development and maintain Garinish as one of the show pieces of Irish gardening.

On arrival a guide book may be purchased which sets out the trail to be followed as well as the plants to be seen between marked stations on this trail. This brochure is an excellent guide, but really unusual or outstanding plants will be highlighted here, while also giving mention to good plants which will adapt to less suitable climatic conditions.

The North Bed beside this old tennis lawn contains a fine specimen of the tender New Zealand pine *Agathis australis* and the Australasian *Acacia baileyana*, a greenhouse shrub in the colder parts of the country. Another New Zealand shrub *Hoheria sexstylosa*, with its showy white flowers in May, is just hardy enough to attempt anywhere, but their soft bark will not withstand really severe frosts. Just as showy as any of the foregoing is the *Camellia japonica* "Adolphe Audusson", a deep blood-red which will grow anywhere given some shade. In the left hand border *Myrtus apiculata* attracts both with its cinnamon-coloured bark and its massed white flowers in late summer with black edible berries to follow in autumn.

Here also is the outstanding *Mahonia lomariifolia* with pinnate leaves 22 inches long and scented yellow flowers, a native of Burma and West China but just hardy in all but the coldest areas. Some may fancy the yellow flowered *Piptanthus laburnifolius*, flowering earlier than the common *Laburnum* and relatively hardy. Across the lawn ericas are dotted over the mown slopes, a setting in which these plants seem out of place, but perhaps pleasing in effect to some beholders.

Passing through the wistaria-covered cassita, built of the soft apricot stone quarried near Bath, the Italian garden is reached where the centre pool has as its four compass points venerable representatives of the Bonsai art. Perhaps this is best viewed in autumn, when the priceless 300-year-old *Larix*, fittingly enshrined in a Roman marble vase, shows its golden autumn colouring. In the borders surrounding the area are many interesting plants. This setting seems to suit the Japanese sacred bamboo, *Nandina domestica*, many of which are seen here, their red-tinted foliage and terminal panicles of white flowers harmonise well.

The *Abutilon* "Ashford Red", a shade of crushed strawberry, will be everybody's envy, but these plants are tender and even here have to be covered in winter. Just within the range of any gardener with a south-facing wall are the white scented rhododendrons "Princess Alice" and "Lady Alice Fitzwilliam" growing along with *R. taggianum* which is the most difficult of the three. Another little-seen shrub present here is *Vestia foetida* from Chile, related to *Cestrum*, but much hardier. The flowers come in mid-summer, tubular in shape and yellowish in colour. A strong shrub of *Grevillea sulphurea* with its striking sulphur-yellow racemes reveals just how favoured this locality must be for these tender Australian subjects to succeed.

Leaving this pleasant little miniature garden and moving out into the open spaces that lead to the finest example of Peto landscaping talent, the Cedar Bed area is entered where *Leucothoe fontanesiana* can be seen carrying its white flowers in short racemes in May and giving a beetroot colour effect in autumn and winter. *Clethra arborea*, yet another shrub carrying white flowers in racemes, is the most tender of its genus coming from Madeira. There is another form of this same species with double flowers under the name of *C. arborea* "Flore Pleno".

In the adjoining bog-bed one cannot pass *Pieris formosa* var. *forrestii*. This particular plant carries a Forrest number of F 27518 which may make it something special though this number does not correspond with that usually regarded as the best of the Forrest introductions named "Charles Michael" and carrying the number F 27765. However any of the *P. formosa* plants are worth having with their brilliant red spring foliage, as striking as any *Rhododendron*, and a bonus of flowering racemes of white, scented flowers. Although not completely hardy, no one should be discouraged from trying this delectable plant; the origins of its name lie in Pieria, the home of the Muses.

Now the greatest vista of the whole island, unimaginatively named Happy Valley, comes into view. This runs almost the entire length of the island terminating at one end in a Grecian temple, the steps leading to it flanked by two rows of Italian cypresses (*Cupressus sempervirens*), and at the other is the famous Martello tower.

Between these two points and divided by a green carpet of close mown lawn live a vast galaxy of plants collected from all parts of the world. Here can be met *Rhododendron yakushimanum*, only found on a small mountainous island close to Japan. Introduced in 1934, it has won every *Rhododendron* award, as befits its shell-pink buds opening to pure white, set in glossy green leaves with a silver underside. The official guide describes this plant as a miniature, but given good conditions it will make a very large miniature, though this may depend upon the individual plant since three distinct types of foliage were discovered in its native habitat of Yakushima. Much more will still be heard about this *Rhododendron*, as its hybrids are only now appearing on the market in numbers. The best of these is perhaps the cross made with *R. haematodes*. Those two much admired Australasian pines, *Dacrydium franklinii* from Tasmania and the equally graceful *D. cupressinum* from New Zealand, must rank among the most handsome conifers in the world. The latter here gets an ideal background of rock outcrop. In late summer the *Eucryphia* will be covered with masses of delicate white flowers showing conspicuous stamens. They are well represented with several species, the best of which is perhaps *E. lucida* with its scented pendulous flowers. Stepping stones lead across to the pond crowded with water lilies, beyond which is a good specimen of the golden larch, *Pseudolarix amabilis*, a slow growing Chinese conifer which unfortunately demands a lime-free soil, perhaps the reason why this conifer is so seldom seen.

In springtime the rhododendrons here dominate the scene; the always exciting *R. arboreum*, brilliant red and of tree size, does not overshadow the smaller members of the family represented by *R. racemosum*, with tiny leaves and small coral-rose flowers; and the pendulous flesh-pink, tubular flowers of that wonderful *cinnabarinum* hybrid "Lady Rosebery" raised at Exbury. There are countless more species and hybrids to be seen here and in the Jungle on the left, but none more accommodating than the miniature *R.*

impeditum which covers itself in tiny violet-coloured flowers and is completely hardy.

So far no mention has been made of the *Embothrium* dotted here and there along the route. Just before the approach to the Martello tower a plant of this Chilean shrub with its intense scarlet display of flower is something that will stop anyone in their tracks. It does seem that the intensity of colour of these shrubs is better in the Cork area than anywhere else. The one here is *E. coccineum* var. *longifolium*, the best certainly but not the hardiest of the genus. Anyone in heavy frost areas should not consider this variety but try instead *E. coccineum* "Norquinco Form", which is perfectly hardy.

Opposite this is another rhododendron easy to grow even in moderate lime. This is *R. callimorphum* which has attractive flowers, red-tinged in bud and changing to deep and light shades of mauve. On this same side by contrast there grows one of the most demanding and difficult plants of Californian origin. This is *Lyonothamnus floribundus* var. *asplenifolius* which could be mistaken for a miniature redwood, having a slender trunk with chestnut coloured bark of soft shaggy tissues. The flowers in May are creamy white. A climb to the Martello tower before leaving provides a panoramic view of this superb feat of landscaping.

Finally, a peep into the old walled garden, supposedly an adjunct to the never built mansion, is very worth while. The fine brick lined walls reveal the high standards of masonry employed in their construction. They now lend support to a number of *Clematis* species and hybrids, mostly popular varieties though including the very lovely large rich pink "Hagley Hybrid".

Climbing and species roses are another feature; and here are included several rugosas with the superb "Roseraie de l'Hay" whose long pointed purplish red buds are resplendent in a setting of massed green foliage. A group of hybrid "Musks" include "Penelope" and "Felicia".

A very interesting and probably early planting is that of *Michelia doltsopa* against the south facing wall. This shrub is now known to be much hardier that at one time credited. Its quality and beauty is beyond question, and the white, heavily scented multi-petalled flowers offer comparison with the magnolias. A splendid specimen planted in the open may be seen in Mrs Walker's captivating garden at Fernhill, Co Dublin. Another rather exceptional item along the centre walk is the variegated *Pittosporum*. This variety with pink tinged margins to its silver leaves is *P. tenifolium* "Garnettii."

This garden has used to the full the very special plant-growing conditions which its geographical position and favoured climate provide. The collection contains many plants seldom seen in other gardens.

Glenveagh National Park

County Donegal

Glenveagh National Park, Co Donegal
Telephone: 074 / 37088

Drive west from Letterkenny for 5 miles (8 Km). Turn right on
to the Church Hill road and proceed north for about 12 miles
(20 Km), following signposts for Castle and National Park.

Glenveagh, one of the more recent additions to our National Parks, has been open to the public since 1984. It is different in many ways from the Killarney and Connemara national parks, but most noticeable is its total isolation. Set in the bleak, mountainous heartland of Donegal, its 25,000 acres now support over 600 red deer. Rock-studded mountain slopes tower above the lake beside which the castle, surrounded by its gardens, was built.

The first to settle here and build this castle fortress was John George Adair, who set out to acquire a sporting property around 1859. In Glenveagh he found a lake containing salmon, and mountains to which deer could be introduced, with perhaps a nucleus stock already present. Seven years later the building of the castle began and this was completed in 1873. His period of residence at the castle was troubled by a poor relationship with his tenants, local feeling having been inflamed by his introduction of Scottish sheep to the hills in 1861. As a result of mounting problems, Mr Adair began to evict his tenants, and thirty families had been dispossessed of their homes by the time of his death.

John Adair's wife was the daughter of a wealthy American Civil War general. Her money had paid for the purchase of the property and she continued to live in the castle after her husband's death. She won back the favour of the local people and then turned her attention to developing the gardens around the castle. Mrs Adair was responsible for much of the large-scale design of the Glenveagh gardens and she planted many trees which provided shelter for later plantings of more tender subjects. She also developed Glenveagh as a Scottish-style deer forest, importing red deer from various sources. The deer book with all the records of the purchases still exists.

Mrs Adair died in 1921 and the estate was purchased in the late 1920s by Arthur Kingsley Porter, a professor from Harvard. He had little horticultural impact on Glenveagh, and following his death, which occurred in rather mysterious circumstances, his widow negotiated the sale of Glenveagh to a wealthy American, Henry P. McIlhenny, who took up residence in 1937.

At the outbreak of the Second World War Mr McIlhenny left Ireland to serve in the US navy, returning to Glenveagh when he was demobilised in 1946. He remained in periodic residence until 1980 and contributed a great deal to both the formal and informal planting in the gardens, partly under the guidance of eminent landscape architects such as James Russell and Lanning Roper. However, as the cost of keeping up the estate began to increase rapidly, Mr McIlhenny entered into negotiations with the Irish government. The Office of Public Works targeted Glenveagh as a National Park, and in 1974 a purchase agreement was reached whereby Mr McIlhenny retained sporting rights and ownership of the castle and gardens, while the title deeds for the rest of the estate passed to the Office of Public Works. In 1980 the castle and environs were conveyed to the government by deed of gift and the private ownership of Glenveagh was terminated.

Glenveagh now finds itself in a similar situation to Muckross House: both are stately homes and gardens surrounded by the wild beauty of national parks. The gardens at Glenveagh have been especially favoured in having the services of a number of very dedicated grounds staff, who have enthusiastically sought to maintain and develop the planting schemes.

The development of the park and gardens has proceeded rapidly during the past ten years. Visitors to the park arrive at a modern but unobtrusive centre where videos and displays give information on the history, geology and natural history of the National Park. Laboratory facilities have been established for those using the park as a centre for research. A small fleet of minibuses conveys visitors from the reception centre up the two-mile avenue to the castle and its gardens; vehicular access to the estate is mercifully restricted.

Someone in Glenveagh must have loved rhodendrons, as some of the worthiest representatives of the genus are to be found here. Many date from the plantings made by Mrs Adair, espcially those around the Pleasure Grounds, where topsoil brought from further up the valley was used to transform the otherwise steep hillside into a more or less level area containing a lawn garden. Hybrids of *R. griersonianum* abound, with the species itself also present. The orange of *R.* "Fabia" greets one inside the gateway, with the bright "Tally Ho" further along the side of the lawn. Towards the centre of this lawn a forty-foot tall specimen of *R. falconeri* proclaims the age of this garden, as do two massive *Griselinia* further on. The size of these contrasts strangely with that of *Drimys winteri*, which here can only be placed in the category of survivors.

The Pleasure Grounds are given a slightly tropical feel by the Chusan palm *Trachycarpus fortunei* and the tree fern *Dicksonia antarctica* which line some of the walks. Midway along the lawn a lofty *Pseudopanax crassifolius* looks down on its terrestrial companions, which include the very beautiful *R. cinnabarinum* with its long, trumpet-shaped flowers. Like waves on the shore of the lake, there are irregular plantings of *Hosta*, *Astilbe*, *Rodgersia* and the indigenous royal fern.

Among the other treasures of this large lawn garden is a thriving *Eucalyptus coccifera*, seen in full flower in early June. Other eucalypts growing here are the snow gum, *E. niphophila* and *E. pauciflora*. All three are in the hardy class. Other items which make this garden special are the rare and beautiful *Michelia doltsopa* introduced by Forrest in 1918, with strongly scented pale yellow or white flowers; the August-flowering *Gevuina avellana*, its white flowers carried in panicles against a background of apple-green ovate leaves; and the scarcely known *Trochodendron aralioides* which has never become a popular plant, although quite hardy. A large snowdrop tree, *Styrax japonica*, may be seen near the exit from the lawn garden.

The walk running uphill and parallel to the Pleasure Grounds passes a huge 60-foot tall *Griselinia littoralis*. This is the Belgian walk, named in memory of the Belgian soldiers who built it as repayment for their keep while they were convalescing during World War I. Alongside the path are many more splendid rhododendrons, including the tender and heavily scented trio of the leggy *R. lindleyi*, *R.* "Princess Alice" and *R.* "Lady Alice Fitzwilliam," all of which are basically white, two with faint yellow throat markings. Another member of this prestigious group is *R. megacalyx*, a large plant with a five-flowered truss smelling of nutmeg. Draping itself over a large rock is the creeping dogwood *Cornus canadensis*, sometimes included in the genus *Chamaepericlymenum*, which bares its white flowers and red fruits in profusion.

We may cut off this path and climb the Twelve Steps Walk to a vantage point where a view is obtained of the Pleasure Ground shrubs below, and from further along can be glimpsed the brooding castle overlooking the shimmering lake. After rejoining the Belgian Walk the Italianate Terrace is reached, which was constructed in 1966. Here are Italian statues and oil jars, while outside the walls are growing Italian cypresses *Cupressus sempervirens*, and *Metrosideros lucida*. Between here and the castle there are many more rhododendrons, including *R. mollyanum* and *R. macabeanum*. The unusual *Fascicularia bicolor* grows as ground cover among the rocks and woodrush; this is one of very few members of the Bromeliad family that can be attempted out of doors in Ireland, although it still must be regarded as a plant for only the mildest parts of the country.

Beside the castle the formal walled garden is divided into squares edged with neatly clipped box, trained into spirals at each corner. The walled garden was originally used for vegetables for the kitchen, but since the castle is no longer lived in, it now contains a mixture of decorative herbaceous material and vegetables grown as much for their colour and shape as for the table. The garden gives the impression of being a period design, yet was constructed as recently as 1957 under the supervision of Mr McIlhenny. On the walls of the castle a vast

Pileostegia viburnoides spreads its large leaves, the white flowering panicles emerge in late summer.

Another shrub leaving pleasant memories of a visit to this garden is the rose-pink multifloriferous *Syringa* hybrid "Bellicent," of which a massed grouping provides an unforgettable display in the Rose Garden. This garden also contains old shrub roses and an unusual small summer house. The wall of this garden almost hides a pretty *Acer psueudoplatanus* "Brilliantissimum."

The View Garden and the Swiss Walk both offer spectacular vistas of the glen and lake. Between the two walks stands the deer larder, outside which are two blue cedars and a fine *Hoheria populnea*. The Swiss Walk, named in honour of Mr Brugger who was involved in the planning of the gardens, has attractive masses of yellow azaleas. Finally, there is an Italian Garden lined with *Griselinia* hedges and Italian statues, and which also contains the unsurpassable *R. augustinii* and that excellent yellow, *R. lutescens*.

Beyond the castle, a path made in 1989 brings the visitor to a vantage point high above the gardens, where the whole of the Glenveagh valley may be seen in all its wild beauty.

Fernhill

County Dublin

Fernhill, Sandyford, Co Dublin

Telephone: Not Listed

This garden is situated 7 miles (11 Km) south of Dublin on the Dundrum/Enniskerry Road. It is served by bus number 44 from Dublin city centre.

Fernhill spreads itself over 40 acres and receives many thousands of visitors every year. Despite its size and popularity it still retains very much of the atmosphere of a family garden. The ties between the Walker family and their garden are very close. Much of the earlier planting was carried out by the enthusiastic plantsman Ralph J. Walker, who built on the foundation laid by the former owner Judge William Darley. Some of the trees at Fernhill testify to the stewardship of its earlier owners. The towering wellingtonias along the Broad Walk were planted in 1860, while the stately beech overhanging the avenue and the spreading sweet chestnut by the old tennis court are both over 200 years old. Today charge of the garden is in the hands of Mrs Sally Walker who has proved more than worthy of the gift handed down to her by her late husband Ralph. In rather too many gardens owners tend to distance themselves from the visiting public. Here a different and more friendly atmosphere prevails with Mrs Walker always ready and glad to discuss with visitors her favourite plants.

Sited on the perimeter of the city of Dublin beside Sandyford, the garden nestles into a heavily wooded hillside with commanding views across the valley towards Killiney and the sea. This combination of shelter and elevation which place it well clear of frost pockets has probably contributed to the success achieved here of growing many rare and delicate plants.

The best place to commence a tour of this garden is prehaps in the vicinity of the house. Here in an island bed on the gravel frontage may be seen a very fine *Azara microphylla* "Variegata," a native of Chile, with cream speckled leaves and small vanilla scented flowers. Close to the house a large *Colquhounia coccinea* var. *mollis* from the Himalayas bears its scarlet trumpet-shaped flowers in late summer. This shrub is somewhat tender unless wall protection can be provided. Equally tender is the *Rhododendron* "Lady Alice Fitzwilliam" growing close by. This plant will cast its spell on all who pass by, with its alluring heavy scent and white trumpet flowers. Also seen here is the tender Tasmanian shrublet *Correa backhousiana*, carrying small greenish-yellow flowers. In late autumn the display of *Nerine* in many shades is very striking.

Next is the rock garden which is enhanced by the basins of water into which the stream has been carefully channelled. The design laid down around 1900 has been little changed and some of the plants here are not newcomers to the scene. An old tree heath *Erica terminalis* from Corsica is remarkably healthy. It is difficult to know why this *Erica* is not seen more often, as it is very tolerant of chalk soils. Another treasure here is an old plant of *Rhododendron* "Bric-a-Brac" which, like its worthy parents *R. leucapsis* and *R. moupinense*, carries its white flowers in early March. Above, on the old tennis courts, the fast growing *Liriodendron tulipifera* is threatening to envelope a fine specimen of *Acer* "Crimson King."

Moving into the glade where the garden merges with its background of beech woodland interspersed with tall larches and some massive sweet or Spanish chestnut, we find rhododendrons lighting up the scene with their varied brilliant colouring. Perhaps the pride of these is a rich cerise *R. arboreum* presented by Dr David Moore from the Glasnevin Botanical Gardens. At a lower level other plants of this genus flourish, which include the rather unusual *R.* "Prelude", a very pleasing yellow obtained by a crossing of *fortunei* with *wardii*, and a very fine plant of *R. genestierianum* characterised by its dazzling white leaf reverse and plum-purple flowers. But perhaps the most outstanding of all plants here is the conifer *Dacrydium cupressinum*. It will be easily recognised by its graceful pendulous whipcord-like branchlets. This New

Zealand red pine is an important timber tree on both islands, where it reaches heights of 200 feet. Here it is very tender and very slow growing to the extent that few gardens attempt to grow it, preferring the hardier *D. franklinii*.

The descent to the Broad Walk affords a good view of the sentinel redwoods planted at its edge overlooking the valley below. These *Sequoiadendron* planted around 1860 are now topping 130 feet and a *Tsuga heterophylla* among them has reached 79 feet. This Broad Walk was probably constructed at the commencement of the garden in 1850, then owned by the Darley family. Tradition has it that on Sunday afternoons tea was served by the butler down this same Broad Walk, who must have passed by these same redwoods when they were young saplings with the valley empty below them. Now the scene has changed, the valley filled with houses dotted everywhere and the redwoods thrusting into the sky. Below the walk another outstanding shrub commands attention with its sheet of white magnolia-like blossoms. This is a well developed *Michelia doltsopa*, a native of China which must be classed as very tender. Close by a collection of oaks provide attractive autumn colouring, but even better in this respect is a large bush of *Acer nikoense* higher up the slope. This acer is so pleasing that, although uncommon in its native habitat in Japan and central China, it will always command a place in cultivation.

Proceeding further down the Broad Walk a Scots pine, *Pinus sylvestris*, is a record contender at 108 feet. On the opposite side, a Victorian relic in the shape of a laurel lawn is maintained in immaculate condition. By mechanical means the clipping of this very considerable area of laurel can be completed in about a day. Unrelieved, such an expanse might appear dull, but here it is a means of accentuating the beauty of the tree stems scattered throughout the lawn. The retention of this lawn is indicative of the attitude of the garden's owner towards gardening patterns of a past age. Too often one sees the total destruction of such pieces of gardening history. The Victorians did not have the advantage of a multitude of globe trotting plant collectors feeding them with the rich diet of new shrubs and plants that came to later generations. Such new shrubs may be seen a little further down the Broad Walk where a new planting of shrubs comprising *Pieris, Leptospermum, Camellia* and many others shows that this garden, while retaining the best of the past, is not disregarding the new introductions of this century.

Now leaving the Broad Walk, a short climb up the slope brings into view what is always a most breathtaking sight, that of a *Magnolia campbellii* in flower. This *M. campbellii* produced its first flower thirty-five years after its planting in 1947. Some trees have been known to take over forty years before reaching flowering stage. The flowers, when they do arrive, are clear pink about 10 inches in diameter. Close to *M. campbellii* is its variety *mollicomata*, which some botanists would claim to be only geographically different from the type. It was discovered by George Forrest nearly sixty years after the discovery of *campbellii* and flowers twenty years sooner, but carries an inferior mauvy pink flower.

The plantings of this little plateau below the rock outcrop also include a good specimen of the umbrella pine *Sciadopitys verticillata*, named after the umbrella shape of its needle clusters, and the water fir, *Metasequoia glyptostroboides*, a tree so graceful in habit and rich in autumn colour. Around the same area a selection of large-leaved rhododendrons are finding conditions to their liking. *R. sinogrande*, the best of George Forrest's introductions, with its striking fawn indumentum on the lower leaf surface, competes with the equally large leaved *R. falconeri*, the latter bearing creamy yellow flowers in May.

More rhododendrons are to be seen along the path heading towards the house; outstanding of these is *R. dalhousiae*, usually regarded as a greenhouse plant but here thriving and usually carrying a bud crop that should ensure a display of its large tubular white flowers coming into May. This plant has contributed to rhododendron history in that, crossed with *griersonianum*, it produced the hybrid "Grierdal".

Back behind the house, where the stream falls down the hillside and steadies itself in arresting pools, waterside plants prevail. Most spectacular are the *Lysichiton americanus* displaying their rich yellow spathes in early summer. Here, the ideal conditions exist for this plant, which is sometimes difficult to establish. Other lovers of this moisture-laden ground are the candelabra members of the *Primula* genus, seen here in an assortment of shades of red. These once established became quickly naturalised.

Finally, a not unexpected feature of this garden is the enclosed area, not walled but caged in by tall beech hedges all neatly clipped. Obviously, this is an old world garden where fruit, flowers and vegetables were originally produced, and little has changed either in outlay or function today. The *espalier* trained apple trees occupy the same wires against which they were planted perhaps eighty years ago, when gardeners possessed the patience, the time and the skill; all three are needed and a little luck as well, to train trees to this perfection. Still here are the herbaceous borders which housed the same plants many years ago, and in an adjoining plot may be seen a collection of many varieties of roses. Just as it was laid down when this garden was created, there still exists a small *parterre* fashioned with box hedges now kept immaculately clipped with roses planted in the enclosed beds.

Howth

County Dublin

Howth, Co Dublin
Telephone: 01 / 322624

Take the coast road north-east from Dublin for 10 miles (16 Km) to the seaside village of Howth. It is served by bus number 31 from Dublin city centre and by the Dart (electric train) from the southside, the city centre or any intermediate station.

Memories of my first visit to Howth many years ago still linger nostalgically. It was on a day in mid-April when steady drizzle prevailed and I and my companion, who at the time had charge of the *Rhododendron* collection at Headfort, were hardly aware of the rain until at the conclusion of our tour we realised our soaking condition. But we had seen this wonderful collection of rhododendrons, many of tree size, under conditions similar to those in their natural forest habitat, with the water-glazed blooms scintillatingly beautiful in the fitful sunlight.

What is it that makes this garden so special and compelling, a garden that offers nothing other than its collection of rhododendrons? Probably firstly, its siting on a cliff face rising 500 feet above sea level which gives the viewer an eyeful of colour such as can never be achieved in any other type of garden. But of equal importance is the fact that this genus of plants can provide every shade of colour, and given the numbers on view here this colour range is on an unprecedented range.

Planting started here around 1850 under the direction of Lady Emily St Lawrence whose garden staff carried soil in sacks up this steep mountainside to begin the first plantings, almost exclusively *R. ponticum* in shades of purple. Nowadays these are considered unattractive and even undesirable by virtue of their dominance over the more colourful but constitutionally weaker later introductions.

Indeed today much of the routine work here consists of checking the growth and uprooting the seedlings and layers of these early *ponticum* plantings. Since then the rate of planting over a long period has been monumental. It is reckoned there have now been planted around 2,000 different varieties of rhododendrons. These include 400 species out of a total of around 800 known to exist. This figure should satisfy those *Rhododendron* purists who tend to view the hybrid introductions with undisguised condescension. Maybe this outlook has been partly brought about by the influence of the Royal Botanic Garden Edinburgh with its strong bias towards the species, probably derived from the close relationship with that famous Scottish collector, George Forrest, who sent all his Sikkim species to Edinburgh. However, if planting were to be confined to species the range of colour at Howth would be much diminished.

Today, access to Howth has been rendered considerably easier with the construction of a road the whole length of the new golf course to the hotel which lies just below the *Rhododendron* hillside. Formerly a path nearly a mile long gave viewers a long walk before the rhododendrons were reached. Now only about fifty yards of this old *Prunus* lined lane remains.

A feature which has always aroused interest along the approach driveway is the encased elm tree opposite the castle. This elm, roughly 400 years old, carried a tradition that when its last bough fell the Howth title would come to an end. So it came about that when the last Earl of Howth died, the last large branch even though anchored by chains came crashing down. Now only the huge old trunk remains with a few small branchlets sprouting from it and even this remnant is threatened with extinction by Dutch elm disease, the attempt to prolong its life with injections of Benomyl having apparently failed.

On entering the rhododendron area the route to the right known as the Rhododendron Walk should be followed. Here at the start are 15 feet high bushes of the Chinese *R. decorum* with pale green glabrous leaves and white to shell-pink flowers. In front of these are *R. crinigerum*, one of George Forrest's introductions. Close by is the rather rare *R. recurvoides*, recognised by its narrow rugose leaves revealing its white pink-tinged flowers. Further along comes the deep scarlet display of the good-tempered *R. neriiflorum* accompanied by *R. sperabile* of similar colour but having rather smaller flowers.

By contrast these have for their near neighbour a bush of the pale cream yellow *R.* "Dairymaid," a hybrid of the magnificent *R. campylocarpum.* More variety is added by the blue of *R. augustinii* and the paler mauve of *R. yunnanense,* a species hardy anywhere, free flowering and able to withstand wind.

Taking a break from the colour scene and turning down the short path to the right leads to a Cromlech, a very remarkable piece of engineering skill belonging to the neolithic age of around 2,000 B.C. This tomb consists of supporting stones twelve feet high, on top of which was placed a flattened slab eight feet in thickness and estimated to weigh 70 tons. Little wonder that this huge weight has over the years caused the partial collapse of its supports.

Another good red here is "Ascot Brilliant", a hybrid of *R. thompsonii,* and a plant of long-proven hardiness. Two of the large leaved varieties are sited just a little way up the path. *R. praestans,* a Himalyan species with magenta-rose flowers is on the left with *R. falconeri* from the central Himalayas on the other side of the path. Beyond these stood the pride of this whole collection, *R.* "Victorianum," a hybrid between *R. dalhousiae* and *R. nuttallii* first made over 100 years ago when both parents were regarded as greenhouse plants. Unfortunately this plant was recently killed by the snow and may be no longer in cultivation in Ireland. As the end of this path is reached two dwarf blues, *R.* "Blue Tit" and *R.* "Blue Diamond," having *R. augustinii* as a common parent come into flower earlier than the backing group of *R.* "Tally-Ho," a first class pink with *R. griersonianum* parentage.

As the path rises towards the summit there my be seen a large plant of "Cornish Cross" on the right, a reliably hardy *griffithianum* hybrid with bell shaped flowers of delicate pink; and on the left that excellent small-flowered yellow *R. xanthocodon,* a plant refined in every sense both in leaf and purity of colour, but not altogether hardy. At a higher elevation *R. insigne* looks distinctive with narrow olive green leaves, grey underneath, and white and pink flowers carrying a darker pink line down the outside of the petals.

The Mountain Walk is aptly named as the climb becomes steeper but the effort is well rewarded by the sight of the exquisite *R*. "May Day". This hybrid between *R. grierson-ianum* and *R. haematodes* must be regarded as perhaps the best of the *griersonianum* crosses. It is completely hardy and not subject to bark splitting, as are so many of these hybrids. The flowers produced in early May are a shade of orange-red, with large calyces of the same colour.

Close by is another of the *griersonianum* hybrids. This time the other parent is *R*. "Venator", the cross having been made at the Marquis of Headfort's garden near Kells and named "Vanguard." The flowers are a brilliant blood scarlet carried on stiffer stems and rather later to open than "May Day".

The return journey to the point of entry may be made by the Soldier's Path running parallel to but at a higher elevation than the Rhododendron Walk, and so providing occasional views of the flowering tops of the tree-size rhododendrons below. It was along this passageway that a very heavy snowfall in 1982 caused the heaviest losses to this collection. The weight of snow caused many to be torn from their roots and while a few have shown regenerative growth, some irreplaceable items have been lost.

It is fortunate that many of the notable plants along this walk have escaped injury. A tree sized *R. calophytum* remains firmly anchored displaying its large, compact, maroon blotched, white flowers. This Chinese species is just about the hardiest of the large leaved varieties, and crossed with "Loderi" has produced that superb hybrid *R*. "Avalanche". Another conspicuous plant here is *R. fulgens*, its young shoots very showy with their crimson bracts. The flowers are a bright scarlet, but it is rather slow to flower. In early April the crimson flowering *R. mallotum* has remarkable leaves with a rich cinnamon-red indumentum. *R*. "Lady Chamberlain", which appears in ten different shades of waxy orange, is seen here in one of its most attractive forms. This hybrid raised at Exbury by Lionel de Rothschild must earn him undying fame.

While the wonderful display of colour is the big attraction here it must be said that the complete lack of labelling may be a disappointment. It will not worry the majority of visitors who will flock to see the unrivalled display of exotic colour. Nor will it dampen the enthusiasm of the knowledgeable band who will enjoy guessing the parentage of some of these interesting hybrids, but in between these groups there are a lot of gardeners who would appreciate being told what they are looking at.

National Botanic Gardens

Dublin

National Botanical Gardens, Glasnevin, Dublin
Telephone: 01 / 374388

Situated in Glasnevin 2.5 miles (4 Km) north of Dublin city centre. Served by buses number 13 and 19 from the city.

The Dublin National Botanic Gardens were originally administered by the Royal Dublin Society which acquired the present site in 1790. The gardens became the property of the State in 1877 and are today, in their enlarged area of 48 acres, under the control of the Department of Agriculture.

Visitors unaware of the soil conditions and the additional hazards of climate and pollution might be deceived into thinking that this is an ideal location for all plants, which indeed it is not. Only the expertise of the staff permits the growing of such subjects as rhododendrons, camellias and heathers in specially prepared sites.

A short distance left of the entrance a large *Parrotia persica* is covered in early spring with dark crimson flowers. A small walled garden on the left used to contain an alpine house in disrepair. The wall plantings include *Corylopsis sinensis* with lemon yellow flowers and *Chimonanthus praecox* "Grandiflorus" also yellow-flowered with a red stain. Both of these flower in early spring. Outside the entrance, the rare Chinese *Neolitsea sericea* has very unusual fawn-brown young leaves of suede-like texture with an underlay of white silk.

Further along a large lawn plot is devoted to a collection of Rosaceae including *Pyrus*, *Malus* and *Sorbus*. A stranger to this collection, the large *Zelkova carpinifolia* midway along the pathway, is closely related to the elms but has a smooth bark and offers a very considerable resistance to the Dutch Elm disease.

A stroll through the lawn collection reveals the wide range of leaf shape and autumn colour in both leaves and fruit. *Pyrus nivalis* is unrivalled in its spring display of white flowers and woolly white leaves. Here is also the elegant willow-leaved pear *P. salicifolia* in its best weeping form. *Malus* is represented by a hybrid raised in the Arnold Arboretum U.S.A., *M. X arnoldiana* with fragrant red-budded flowers followed by yellow-red flushed fruits. A rich variety of *Sorbus* includes *S. anglica* from the Aria section. In Ireland, this may be found growing in the wild only around Killarney. *Sorbus cashmiriana* has everything to commend it, leaves both large and elegant, and flowers of delicate pink, followed by translucent white fruits which remain on the tree long after leaf-fall. Nor should mention be omitted of the Chinese rowan *Sorbus pohuashanensis* which in autumn carries such a weight of fruit that its branches bend into looping cascades of orange red.

Further along behind a pergola of *Clematis*, the magnolias enjoy a corner of comparative shelter. The rare *M. fraseri* with leaves of up to 16 inches long carries large, scented white flowers. The splendid *M. grandiflora* is represented here by the cultivar "Ferruginea" with large cream and white flowers and leaves showing the rust coloured undercoating from which the name is derived. Across the path a 40-foot *Robinia pseudacacia* makes a splendid show when in mid-summer it is covered in faintly scented, white-yellow stained flowers. Beside it *R. X hillere* reveals itself as a better specimen for the smaller garden. The flowers are a slightly more pinkish hue.

The oak wood can hardly be missed and nothing else but a wood can describe this assemblage of oaks from many corners of the world. Perhaps the planting is rather overcrowded but who would deny any one of these trees its right of inclusion. Names seldom heard crowd all around you. *Quercus fragrans* of unknown origin has flowers of unusual fragrance, a characteristic also pertaining to its timber. The variegated Turkey oak *Q. cerris* "Variegata" has long toothed variegated leaves and has woolly acorn cups. The purely ornamental varieties are well represented and include the quite rare *Q. X turneri* thought to be a hybrid between *Q. ilex* and *Q. robur*, which is evergreen with small acorns on long stalks.

The compact *Q. phillyreoides* is another rare evergreen,

seldom here reaching more than bush size but occasionally reaching tree size. Some splendid autumn colour is provided by *Q. rubra,* whose red colouring is comparable to the slightly deeper shades of *Q. coccinea.* Another unusual note is provided by *Q. phellos*, a willow-leaved oak from the U.S.A. with smooth bark, but rarely producing acorns in these islands. On the very edge of this beautiful oak glade stands perhaps the most illustrious oak of all. Here the tortuous shape of that uniquely commercial tree, the cork oak, the only tree supplying this major domestic requirement, displays its cork lined limbs. *Q. suber* is a native of the Iberian peninsula and introduced to Spanish America, where the best cork producing trees are stripped of their bark every ten years.

The border along the wall leading towards the conifer area contains some interesting plants. An *Acacia melanoxylon* is developing with the aid of kind winters. Another tender plant seen in very few Irish gardens, *Maytenus boaria,* has reached a commanding size. The foliage of this plant is said to be very seductive to cattle. A Wilson introduction, the Chinese *Pseudopanax davidii* of borderline hardiness is only listed in two other gardens in the country. This area also contains a rather unusual relation of the ash, *Fontanesia phillyreoides.* The flowers borne in June are greenish-white. This section of the garden may well have a greater appeal for the connoisseur than for the average gardener.

Passing along to the conifers which are reasonably well represented, it should be realised that a pollution problem has a bearing on the performance of some. Pride of place probably goes to the magnificent *Pinus montezumae.* Too often the more easily grown *P. montezumae* var. *hartwegii* is used as a substitute, but this is much greener than the type. Another Mexican, *Pinus ayacahuite,* can also be seen here, again distinguished by its glaucous colouring. An interesting comparison is offered by the close planting of *Pinus pinea* and its cultivar "Fragilis". This species must rank as a very early introduction as it is known to have been brought over by the Romans who regarded its seeds as quite a delicacy.

The larch section on the edge of this plantation contains

some interesting trees. The two Siberian larches *Larix gmelinii* and *L. sibirica*, the latter having bark capable of being processed into fine quality white gloves, are not well suited to British climatic conditions, opening their buds too early to escape late frosts, but here both have reached a reasonable size. Nearby the Chinese tulip tree does not have too much to commend it. The leaves are narrower, the flowers are smaller and the colour duller than the more frequently seen American species. *Diospyros duclouxii* is something of a rarity. The director of the gardens, Mr Aidan Brady, states that this specimen was obtained from Hilliers in 1941 costing 4/9d and that it came from a Chinese collection. A rather sickly *Pinus morrisonicola* provides confirmation of the problems associated with the growing of this conifer elsewhere.

The rhododendron collection provides a good range of colour in Spring and early Summer. Unsatisfactory soil conditions render difficult the growing of many of the more outstanding varieties. There are included a few rare species such as *R. detonsum* carrying large pink tresses in May and *R. anthosphaerum*, a campanulate crimson or magenta. An unusual plant is featured by *R. ponticum* "Cheiranthifolium" with its narrow wavy leaves. Those species and hybrids popular in most gardens are also in evidence here.

The gardens contain several glasshouses including some magnificent relics of the curvilinear design age which in later years have fallen into an advanced state of disrepair. A government grant has now been approved for their restoration which hopefully can be achieved despite the corrosion which has penetrated much of the metal work. Sections of the range of glasshouses are still in reasonable order, including the orchid house, containing many items of interest. Included in this collection are the minutely speckled emperor purple *Odontioda* "Drumbeat", the white-lipped *Cattleya trianae,* and most regal of all, the white star flower of that Madagascar introduction *Angraecum sesquipedale.*

In the fern house the famous if unspectacular Killarney fern *Trichomanes speciosum* is housed in a damp grill-barred grotto. Among the stately tree ferns *Dicksonia antarctica* holds a prominent position. In close proximity is the most venerable fern in the country, *Todea barbara*, which was sent from Melbourne in 1892 to Trinity College Botanic Garden. On the transfer of these gardens to their present site, it was presented to Glasnevin in 1969. It is claimed that this plant is now 300 years old.

The herbaceous presence in this establishment is confined to twin borders divided by a box edged walk of 100 yards filled with a limited variety of herbaceous plants commonly grown in Irish gardens. Above this a rockery of a further 60 yards presents rockery and alpine plants.

The gardens are open every day except Christmas Day during advertised hours.

Talbot Gardens
(Malahide Castle)

County Dublin

Talbot Gardens, Malahide Castle, Malahide,
Co Dublin
Telephone: 01 / 542337

Situated 9 miles (14.5 Km) north of Dublin. Served by number 42 bus from Dublin city centre. Malahide Castle is on the Dublin side of Malahide village.

Malahide Castle and gardens are now owned by Dublin County Council, this body having purchased the property in 1977 from the executors of the estate of the late Lord Talbot de Malahide, who was a recognised authority on Australasian plants and accumulated a large collection of them at Malahide. Dublin County Council have now preserved the remnants of this collection and are endeavouring to introduce some of the items lost before they obtained possession.

The visionary action of the council in spending a sum of money approaching three quarters of a million pounds must be regarded as a brave decision, but one fully justified when viewed against the probable total loss of this national heritage had the estate been permitted to pass into the hands of developers. The estate is now classified as a regional park, having the dual role of providing local recreational facilities and as an addition to Dublin's tourist attractions.

On its reopening, problems occurred within the confines of the very important walled garden containing most of the rare plants, some of which were removed or destroyed by vandals. Temporary closure of this portion of the garden from the general public became necessary. Now the position has improved and the walled garden is open from 2.00 p.m. on Wednesday afternoons for individuals taking part in conducted tours, and to societies by appointment.

The open portion of the garden lies mostly on the northerly side of the castle, whose walls provide protection for some of the more tender shrubs and climbers. Best of these is a *Magnolia grandiflora*, whose large creamy-white fragrant flowers sometimes ten inches in diameter continue through the summer. Filling the view from the Castle windows is a massive oak, *Quercus petraea*, of no rarity but very picturesque in the spring when its shapely limbs which slant downwards to ground level shelter the massed snowdrops, which encircle the tree as a white carpet.

In spring this garden is decorated by its many viburnums, including *V. X burkwoodii*, and *V. carlesii*, both being among the most fragrant of the genus. Crinodendrons also do well and both *C. hookerianum* with dark crimson lantern shaped flowers, and the later white-flowered *C. patagua* flower freely. The garden form of *Podocarpus macrophyllus* "Aureus" makes an attractive large bush in a setting which shows its golden colour to the best advantage.

It is perhaps surprising to see *Desfontainia spinosa* with its striking orange-red tubular flowers thriving so well in this limestone soil. Flowering in July it fills a rather lean period. A large peat bed planted with Kurume azaleas shaded by high trees reveals the ambitions of Lord Talbot in attempting these rather difficult subjects in a soil entirely unsuitable. The experiment has yet to succeed.

Proceeding eastward, the garden's main axis of a broad grass walk provides a vista from castle to golf course. At the latter end of this strip are two twin *Juniperus recurva* var. *coxii*. These graceful weeping trees would be seen to better effect if less enclosed. Nearby a *Podocarpus andinus* is enjoying both the lime and the shading. The flaming red leaves of *Photinia serratifolia* are the chalk garden's answer to the challenge of *Pieris* on acid soils. Several of these colourful shrubs are dotted around this garden. The accommodating but little grown *Stachyurus* is represented here by *S. praecox*, a large growing shrub with racemes of pale yellow flowers and rich purple leaf shading.

The Tasmanian cedars are well represented here by the three species which comprise the genus, *Athrotaxis*; *A. selaginoides*, the largest of the three, *A. laxifolia* and *A. cupressoides*. Another striking conifer is *Chamaecyparis lawsoniana* "Wisselii", columnar in shape and outstanding in spring when covered with red male strobili.

Two interesting *Ribes* may attract some interest. The very dwarf *R. laurifolium* makes an excellent rock garden plant with greenish white flowers in spring and red berries in autumn. The other is *R. fasciculatum* which bears creamy yellow flowers in dense racemes. The rare Himalyayan conifer *Abies spectabilis*, very susceptible to spring frosts, is growing along one of the side walls. The young shoots are reddish brown and the cones are violet.

The setting of this garden is beautiful, its plants are most carefully tended and the labelling is near perfect on all except still unidentified subjects. Before leaving, a brief visit to the old main entrance drive will be rewarding since here are some outstanding plants.

A very well formed *Drimys winteri* will be noticed on the right facing the entrance gates, and on the other side it is most remarkable to find the tender *Hakea* bearing white brush-like flowers freely. The species here is *H. lissosperma*.

The closed garden contains a much wider and rarer range of plants. Many originals of the Lord Talbot era were lost, but replacements for these are being sought and many have been obtained. One advantage of the Lord Talbot connection is that links formed with botanical gardens throughout the world have never been severed and this source of supply is still open.

This section of the gardens comprises one large walled garden, originally the kitchen garden, within which are a number of smaller areas enclosed by walls. The first of these has high walls sheltering its choice collection of plants.

The Chinese *Clematis macropetala*, producing in late May three inch flowers of violet blue with inner staminodes of paler blue, is strikingly effective. A more difficult plant, seldom seen, is *Cassia obtusa* which has terminal clusters of rich yellow flowers in late summer. The plant, coming from tropical America, usually requires conservatory accommodation.

The large leaved *Azara petiolaris* fills the surrounding air with its heavy scent. The dwarf conifer *Picea abies*, probably the form "Gregoryana", rises in perfect symmetry, layer by layer to a height of around ten feet. With one of the lowest growth rates this tree could be expected to reach its present height in about 20 years. Unusual rather than attractive, the white flowered *Ceanothus rigidus* does not really equal the appeal of its blue relatives. Another member of this exclusive set is the Tasmanian *Correa lawrenciana*, which I have yet to see in flower.

Passing through the Pond Garden, where more *Ceanothus* give a good display and a superb *Clematis alpina* shows off its violet blue flowers, a tiny enclosure which was formerly a chicken run is reached. It has been converted with extended walls to accommodate some more choice plants. The *Lomatia* most often seen are of Chilean origin, but here can be seen the Tasmanian *L. tinctoria* with sulphur yellow flowers.

A place on the wall has also been found for the southern hemisphere *Aristotelia chilensis*. This evergreen shrub with long lustrous leaves is again a plant only for mild areas. Some rhododendrons are growing here on prepared sites, including the dainty *R.* "Seta" raised at Bodnant, which has almost tubular pink and white flowers.

Next the Tresco Wall, probably originally named and chosen because of its very sheltered location, accommodates the garden's most prized plants. Most of the rarities have been lost but gaps are being filled whenever suitable items come to hand.

From California there is the *Lyonthamnus floribundus* var. *asplenifolius* with soft loose bark like a redwood and *Spiraea*-like flowers in ivory white. A *Feijoa sellowiana* "Mrs Roosevelt" does not appear to have characteristics different from the type. It would be interesting to know its origins. The large walled garden at the other side of the Tresco Wall contains a wide assortment of plants garnered from many parts of the world. A beautiful *Acacia pravissima* with very delicate flowers is of Tasmanian origin. Another wall subject is a large *Fremontodendron* "California Glory" trained like an espalier. The deciduous mimosa *Albizia julibrissin,* also given wall protection, has pink flower heads in summer. The variety "Rosea" is said to be hardier. Mention must also be given to a large plant of *Berberis valdiviana* with holly-like spineless leaves and saffron yellow flowers.

The reserved portion of this garden is so well worth seeing that interested visitors would be well advised to take advantage of its Wednesday tours.

Trinity College Botanical Gardens

Dublin

Trinity Botanical Gardens, Dartry, Dublin 6
Telephone: 01 / 972070

In the pretty suburb of Dartry, these gardens are tucked in behind Palmerston Park, 2.5 miles (4 Km) from Dublin's city centre. Served by number 13 bus (southwards).

The present botanical gardens attached to the College are situated at Trinity Hall, Palmerston Park. They were set up in 1967, and are in direct descent from the previous gardens established by the University around the beginning of the 19th century, then situated at Shelbourne Road. It was at that time the practice for all the householders around the garden square to be granted free admission at any time. This became know as the Keyholders' Club. On Sunday mornings, the club had the gardens to themselves with no staff surveillance. Perhaps it is a reflection of the changes in public morality that today no botanical institution could contemplate admitting any section of the public on trust. That distinguished Irish botanist, James Mackay, author of *Flora Hibernica*, was the first curator of the Ballsbridge gardens. The present gardens, although only 20 years in existence, contain many well established trees, some moved from the previous site.

Beside the entrance are two raised beds, one containing Burren limestone and the other Wicklow granite. These provide contrasting soil types for the wide range of rock garden and alpine species grown here, including a number of the hardy saxifrages. Close by, another bed is devoted to the display of endangered Irish species, including *Helianthemum canum* from the Burren and the Donegal endemic *Saxifraga rosacea* ssp. *hartii*.

The adjoining gardens formerly attached to the Hall still retain their old world atmosphere, with some of the orignal apple trees still healthy and fruitful. No one would suppose this to be a particularly favoured climatic area of Dublin yet here

Melianthus major, a sub-shrub from South Africa of tender reputation, is growing contentedly; its tubular crimson flowers are borne in terminal racemes but equally splendid are the very large deeply notched pinnate leaves.

Two varieties of *Actinidia* adorn the wall, the size and elegance of their leaves placing them well up the list of desirable climbers. The Killarney *Sorbus anglica* looks at its best in autumn when the leaves turn golden brown, forming a perfect backing for its scarlet fruits. Another feature of this old garden is the white-stemmed Himalayan birch, *Betula utilis* "Trinity College", an unusual tree in that some forms have mahogany-brown bark and others the distinctive white. Another tree here with bark appeal is the *Prunus serrula* which has a very limited flower display but excels in the shining mahogany-brown bark covering its standard height stem. The African *Euryops pectinatus* adds a bright touch of colour with its richly yellow daisy-type flowers.

The south arboretum, bordered on one side by the construction site of a large pond in which it is intended to house some of the aquatic endangered species, and a walled border on the other side, contains a large area of lawn filled with specimen trees and shrubs, primarily planted for research purposes but forming as pleasing an assocation as might be found in any garden. A large *Aralia elata* arranges its pinnate leaves in a terminal ruff giving a most picturesque impression, enhanced by its large white panicles of flowers in autumn. The leaf design of the *Meliosma dilleneifolia* makes this a very attractive species, with leaves seven to eight inches long, and carrying panicles of scented yellowish-white flowers. This is a very rare tree indeed.

Another of the botanically interesting trees, the New Zealand *Plagianthus betulinus* with long lanceolate leaves, is related to *Hoheria*. The Turkish hazel *Corylus colurna* features here and unlike most of its genus is strikingly symmetrical in appearance; in addition its bark is fissured in ribs of cork-like tissue. The large black walnut *Juglans nigra* at the top of this garden has no claims to the unusual, but few trees of complete hardiness are more majestic, or can boast of such handsome leaves as those long dark-green pinnate ones displayed by this tree. The one here has yet to bear its large round nuts, unlike the smaller *Juglans regia* nearby. If you are fortunate enough to be visiting this garden in late July the large Tasmanian *Leptospermum lanigerum* (syn. *pubescens*) makes a fine show when covered in its white blossoms.

Two of Roy Lancaster's introductions may be seen here. *Rubus ichangensis*, an upright growing bramble, has a place in the wall border, and a small tree of the Chinese ash, *Fraxinus chinensis*, was raised from seed introduced by him. The fact that this tree is of wild origin adds to its usefulness for research purposes. Its flowers are sweetly scented and its leaves assume plum tints in autumn. This part of the garden contains many more shrubs of unusual interest, and its visitors will be rewarded by a more detailed study of its occupants.

An extensive range of small glasshouses is used to display separately the more delicate flora and to exhibit plants of economic value. One of the smaller houses contains a collection of plants of Irish origin, including *Erica ciliaris* with pink flowers from August to October. This plant occurs locally in South-West Britain and on the continent, but in Ireland is found only at a single site in Connemara. Another Irish rarity given protection here is the cottonweed *Otanthus maritimus,* which has dramatically declined in numbers this century. This house also contains the saxifrage collection, which consists of a large number of mainly European species, mostly of wild origin. Many of these make extremely attractive rock garden subjects, from the tight grey-leaved mounds of *S. caesia* to the huge panicles of *S. longifolia.*

Another small house is devoted to European plants of wild origin, and to tender bulb species. Once again, the emphasis is on conservation, with several endangered species being grown. Seeds of these species are collected annually, and are available for exchange with other botanic gardens and research institutions.

The next greenhouse visited contained a collection of tropical species. Some are familiar as house plants, others much less well known, such as a collection of plants found only on the island of Mauritius. These were collected on an expedition to the island which was organized by the gardens in 1985; the collection includes the very rare *Nesocodon mauritianus*, a very attractive species with large pale purple bell-shaped flowers which contain bright red nectar. A decorative *Passiflora quadrangularis* with large perfumed flowers climbs over the roof supports; this along with *Strelitzia* and the inevitable *Monstera deliciosa* gives a real impression of the humid tropics. Beware of *Acokanthera spectabilis*, the bark of which is used by some jungle dwellers to obtain poison for their arrows.

Anyone interested in collecting cycads and with the means to provide the necessary heat for these tropical or sub-tropical plants can get an introduction to them in a house whose central portion contains a collection of these palm-like plants, with their shaggy trunks of loose fibres topped by clusters of large divided leaves. Cones are produced on both male and female plants. Many of the large specimens are over a hundred years old, but there are also several seedlings of more recent introduction. Another remarkable inmate is *Xanthorrhoea quadrangularis*, otherwise known as the Australian grass tree or black boy. The lowest layer of the needle-like leaves dies back and hangs as a skirt around the trunk; in its natural habitat this burns rapidly in the bush fires, but stimulates flowering. The plant flowered in 1987, without burning! Other plants of note in this house are *Pelargonium*, begonias and bromeliads.

Three small glasshouses are largely taken up with research work and propagation; of more interest to the visitor is the adjacent lean-to glasshouse. One section of this house contains orchids and economically important crops. Some of the orchids are very old, the labels of some showing that they were collected in the last century. In the central part of the house a small coffee tree bears reddish beans, while *Gossypium barbadense* produces fluffy tufts of cotton from its seeds. The ginger plant is deceptively demure, giving no indication of the demon in its roots.

The next section contains a collection of desert and semi-desert plants of all shapes and sizes. Many are contained in a large raised sand bed in the centre of the glasshouse; various species from a wide range of totally unrelated families show similar water-conserving features such as succulent foliage or stems, often with vicious spines. One of the most treasured plants here is *Testudinaria elephantipes* or elephants foot, which has been in the Trinity Gardens for over one hundred years. A shoot is produced each summer from the massive woody rootstock, this grows rapidly and trails about the greenhouse supports. In sharp contrast is the collection of ferns in the next section. Only a small number of species are grown, but these include the graceful *Cibotium schiedei*, and *Todea barbara*, an offshoot from the plant sent to Glasnevin from the original Trinity fernhouse in Ballsbridge, and now over 300 years old. A special case provides the high humidity required by the rare Killarney fern *Trichomanes speciosum*.

Behind the glasshouse lies a long raised bed containing some of the smaller flowering plants and shrubs such as *Hebe*, *Potentilla* and *Erica*. If the wide pathway leading towards Trinity Hall is then followed, a fulsome collection of many of the lesser known shrubs and trees can be viewed in the grass lawns. *Laburnum alpinum*, sometimes referred to as the Scotch laburnum, flowers rather later than the common variety with long racemes of yellow flowers and leaves of a deeper green. The magnificent colouring of *Parrotia persica* is a well known sight, but here is the less usual relation *Parrotiopsis jacquemontiana* which is more rewarding in flower with similar autumn charm. Two unusual conifers are contained in this collection, the Chinese *Picea asperata* and the Californian *Abies bracteata*, distinguished by its bewhiskered cones.

The new plantation adjoining the old college hockey ground is still very young, and here again one does not have to look very far for the unusual. A young and thriving plant of *Nyssa sylvatica* reveals this soil is not over-endowed with lime. The autumn colour of this plant is its special feature but not all specimens seem to oblige in this respect. *Eucommia ulmoides*, the only hardy rubber producing plant, will be a stranger to many visitors although also on show at Birr Castle. Quite a large specimen of the Spanish Fir *Abies pinsapo* seems to be adapting well to its new site, since this is a tree which resents being moved except when very young.

These gardens, although not generally open to the public, do welcome visits by horticultural societies or other interested groups by arrangement. Anyone undertaking such a visit will be well rewarded, as the range here for a small garden is quite outstanding.

Derreen

County Kerry

Derreen Gardens, Lauragh, Kenmare, Co Kerry
Telephone: 064 / 83103

These gardens are situated near Lauragh, some 15 miles (24 Km) south west of Kenmare on the road to Castletownbere.

County Kerry, lying on the extreme south western corner of Ireland directly in the path of the Gulf Stream currents, might be expected to house gardens containing the finest collection of plant life in the country. Few places in the British Isles can boast of a more favourable climate yet only two outstanding gardens are to be found within its boundaries.

Derreen, home of the Hon. David Bingham, is the most remote of all Irish gardens, being situated near the mouth of the Kenmare river with no land to the west nearer than North Newfoundland. Its isolation is emphasized by the terrain through which the visitor passes *en route* from Killarney. The narrow road bends and loops through the foothills of this mountainous area, with scraggy sheep more numerous on the road than motorists.

From the high passes, the almost aerial views down into the distant valleys below reveal a multitudinous quilt of russet browns and mossy greens broken with rock outcrop, so vividly arresting in the unaccustomed wildness of the scenery. Kenmare provides a brief glimpse of civilisation before crossing the river and continuing down the left bank again in solitudinous reverie until Derreen is reached.

Like most Irish gardens Derreen came into existence through Anglo-Irish initiative. In 1690 the land was granted to Sir William Petty, medico to Cromwell's forces, whose daughter married Lord Kerry, this title being later changed to Lord Lansdowne. In the late nineteenth century the fifth Marquis of Lansdowne began to develop the gardening potential of Derreen, aided in this work by the fact that, as

Viceroy of India, he was himself able to supervise the collection of a wide range of Himalayan rhododendrons which contain some of the choicest species of this very large and much appreciated genus.

I visited this garden on a day in late October when a heavy mist hung low overhead, the undergrowth through which one strolled was dripping and puddles had formed along the paths, yet despite the adverse conditions the potential of this place was very evident. At every turning another seascape came into view, there was water everywhere and the rhododendrons were obviously revelling in these moist conditions. With its hundred acres of land available for development, this is comparable to a nature park and completely eclipses its neighbour, Garinish Island, in size. But costs are a factor in gardening these days and one cannot say what sort of expansion can be achieved. At the moment, about fifty new plants are being added each year.

Since rhododendrons form the main display, the best time to visit this garden is in late spring or early summer when the peak flowering period is reached. The *Rhododendron arboreum* on the lawn is the largest in the garden. Records show that 400 of these were planted in 1873. Guide posts direct the visitor as to which routes to follow on this woodland trail, which starts with a view of the magnificent Himalayan plant *R. falconeri*, its large leaves a fitting match for the huge creamy-yellow dome shaped trusses with purple throat blotches; but like all large-leaved plants it demands good shelter.

Another very similar plant also here is *R. sinogrande*, the possessor of the largest leaves of any evergreen grown in these islands with the possible exception of *Magnolia delavayi*. It is of tree size with very dark green leaves on top, shining grey beneath. The floppy trusses may carry up to 20 flowers, creamy-white in colour with a crimson splash at their base. Any attempt to grow this plant, which comes from the low-lying Himalayan rain forest and is therefore tender, may lead to disappointing results since it flowers strictly according to size. This specimen was planted in 1907.

An altogether more adaptable plant growing close by is the hybrid "Temple Belle", a product of those two hardy parents *R.*

orbiculare and *R. williamsianum*. The leaves are a polished green with red veining and the flowers a rosy pink, opening in May. The last of this particular group and perhaps the most delicate is that exquisite hybrid *R.* "Fragantissimum", which as its name implies is heavily scented, with white lemon-stained flowers. It too has Himalayan connections, being a hybrid of the very straggly and tender *R. edgeworthii*. Across the path from these is a good sized *Drimys winteri* which also in May fills the air with its delicately scented white flowers.

Continuing to explore the labyrinth of paths which afford views of the lofty Kerry mountains and the Atlantic Ocean stretching into the horizon, some of the earliest planted mammoth trees will be met. Pride of place must go to the *Pinus radiata* planted in 1880 and now 85 feet high, a record for Ireland, shared with another specimen growing at Hamwood in County Meath. These Monterey pines are distinguished by their exceptionally bright green leaves carried in groups of three, although variable in young trees. A Caucasian fir, *Abies nordmanniana*, is but a foot shorter than the record holder for Ireland growing at Powerscourt.

The pride of Derreen is the unique Japanese cypress, *Cryptomeria japonica* "Elegans", which in its stance and size must command attention from all who view it. This tree met with an accident by being partially uprooted by a storm and now leans across the path in a near horizontal position. Had it remained upright it would have been in a challenging position to the tallest of its kind recorded in the British Isles, which is a tree of 70 feet in Devon, only three feet taller than the 67 feet measurement of this storm victim. The Western red cedar *Thuja plicata* was somebody's fancy here as a number of them, including one compact grove, were planted around 1880 and now stand at around 82 feet, far from record proportions. These are still very majestic trees, distinguished by their shredding cinnamon-coloured bark and odour-emitting leaves.

The mild and moist conditions prevailing beneath these tall trees are ideal for the ferns, many of which are quite outstanding in size and tropical in appearance. The specimens of tree ferns, including some *Dicksonia antarctica* of New

Zealand origin, were planted here in 1900 and are now a commanding size. Other plants to revel in these conditions include the *Gunnera manicata*, a perennial plant which looks rather like a giant rhubarb but with leaves three times the size and having protective bristles on both leaves and stems.

Unnoticed underfoot, but indicative of the moisture laden air, are the tiny feathery mosses called *Thuidium*. So it is no surprise to find here a very shapely specimen of the swamp cypress, *Taxodium distichum*. Perhaps the most beautiful of the conifers, its green graceful appearance during the summer months gives way to an even more alluring display of russet brown colour in autumn. At the end of the lawn below the house, a semi-circular planting contains a mixture of unusual and tender shrubs mixed with some more choice rhodo-dendrons. Among the most noteworthy shrubs are the tender *Acacia melanoxoylon*, a large *Crinodendron hookerianum*, two *Hoheria lyallii* and the Chilean *Myrtus apiculata*, with white flowers in late summer. Also in this area a good example of *Parrotia persica* provides splendid autumn colour.

Another eye catching but easily grown plant seen here is *Stranvaesia davidiana* var. *undulata*, which is rather dwarfer but more spreading than the type. It bears clusters of red fruits hanging in pendulous fashion along the branches and its appearance is further enhanced by a number of its leaves turning cherry red throughout the year.

Less often seen is *Styrax japonica*, best grown in a peaty soil. Its white bell-shaped flowers hang downwards from the branches so that it is best viewed from a lower elevation. Among the acacias growing here *A. melanoxylon* is already a large specimen giving a remarkable display when in flower, with its soft yellow flowers set against the graceful pinnate foliage.

The rhododendrons in this area include that wonderful hybrid "Shilsonii", resulting from the cross between *R. thomsonii* and *R. barbatum*, both of Himalayan origin. The flowering period is intermediate between that of its parents and flowers of waxy blood-red may be expected in late March. A rather hardier but less desirable hybrid *R.* "Loderi", which comes in so many varieties that considerable contention arises as to which is the best, here shows its robust and floriforous habit always covering itself in floppy whitish pink large trusses. The plant here is "Loderi King George". The more discerning grower will probably prefer the cross between this variety and *R. calophytum* called "Avalanche".

Almost escaping notice the little dwarf *R. keiskei* nestles below the giants. This Japanese rock garden species coming from the island of Yakushima set in the sub-tropical China sea, is not hardy in the sense that while its survival is not in question it will only produce its clusters of lemon-white flowers under favourable conditions.

Yet one more rhododendron, perhaps only to be found in this classic collection, is the exceptionally tender *R. zeylanicum* with very dark green leaves and red flowers carried in a dense truss appearing from December to late April. The few examples mentioned may serve to indicate the wide range of this collection of rhododendrons, flowering over a period of three months.

The beauty of this remote garden surrounded by the Atlantic Ocean but sheltered by its extensive timber cover is never absent, but is best discovered in the fullness of the rhododendron season. This remarkable genus, providing colour for more than half the year, is beautiful wherever it is seen, but none more so than in wild remote localities such as here, where these plants are nearest to their natural habitat of montane forest.

Muckross
(Killarney National Park)

County Kerry

Muckross Gardens (Killarney National Park),
Killarney, Co Kerry
Tel: 064 / 31440

The entrance to Muckross House and Gardens is well signposted 3 miles (5 Km) south of Killarney on the road to Kenmare.

The Killarney National Park contains a very wide assortment of interesting plants, some with indigenous traditions, others as a result of wild seeding or planting. This, in combination with the cultivated plant collection contained in Muckross Gardens, makes Killarney a renowned mecca for botanists and plant lovers from both Ireland and abroad. In 1982, its fiftieth year of State ownership, this vast demesne received recognition from UNESCO in naming it a Biosphere reserve, an honour well deserved in view of the richness of its heritage.

The original owners of Muckross in the early 18th century were the Herberts, a Protestant family who earned much respect by their disinclination to evict their tenants, contrasting with the wholesale evictions carried out by their neighbours. Succeeded in 1899 by Lord Ardilaun whose tenure only lasted until 1910, the property then passed into the hands of Arthur Vincent, later Senator, being a gift from his father-in-law, Mr W. B. Bourne. Senator Vincent in turn presented Muckross to the nation in 1932.

The family mansion, Muckross House, a portion of which is used as offices for the Park Administration staff, is open to the public. Downstairs its reception rooms give magnificent far-flung views across the lakes and upstairs its principal bedrooms contain the best furniture on display in the house. Most of the outstanding items of furniture were stripped from the mansion to aid the furnishing of Irish embassies abroad. The house, unfortunately, does not match the antiquity of its surroundings; built by the Herberts in the 19th century it is just one of four that have existed here. The other three, one close to the shores of Lough Leane, all preceded it. However, its landscaped gardens do reveal the potential of this locality for growing plants of imported origin which can only survive in specially favoured areas.

If Mr Carson, the horticultural supervisor, were to have his way, he would have every visitor come to the park at daybreak so they would not miss seeing the sunrise on *Eucalyptus cordata*. This worthy plant is the pride of his eye and no one meeting him will be left in any doubt about its virtues. This south Tasmanian plant found growing at medium altitudes should be hardier than in fact it is; fortunately it has the endearing habit of flowering at an early age, and its leaves undergo no changes between the juvenile and adult forms. Tasmanian gardeners have discovered the merits of this *Eucalyptus* as a summer bedding plant. The tree may also be seen at Fota Island and at that famous hotel garden nearby, Ashbourne House.

Mr Carson proclaims that the temperature here is only slightly colder than at Garinish Island which explains the presence of a splendid specimen of *Melaleuca gibbosa*, a very tender Australian plant rather similar to the bottle brushes. Less fortunate is its rainfall, which at 67 inches is so high that in the natural rockery below the house alpines will not survive.

On the wide stone plateau set in rock outcrop overlooking the old tennis court, the tennis players of another era enjoyed their afternoon tea. History being but a recording of past memories, this is part of the history of this great garden carved from a rough landscape by the family who lived here.

Set at the bottom of this high tiered rock garden one alpine is defying the rains. This is *Haberlea ferdinandi-coburgi*, a plant related to the *Ramonda* with rosette-shaped evergreen leaves and mauve flowers in early spring. Two shrubs here make a very considerable contribution to the autumn colour scene. *Euonymus alatus* is a small growing member of this large genus which provides a quite brilliant display of autumn colour, with an additional character trait of having rather unusual cork ribs along its branches. The other is *Acer palmatum* var. *heptalobum* "Osakazuki" which provides a fiery scarlet autumn colour of unsurpassable richness. This *Acer* can sometimes be sulky and difficult to establish but here it is expressing complete satisfaction with its surroundings.

In late springtime the central area of this garden comes alive with colour when the huge clumps of rhododendrons burst into bloom, displaying all the shades which this magnificent genus of plants is capable of providing. In their midst stands a grove of Scots pine, a tree that always looks well-chosen when placed in just such a position with large-sized rhododendrons. The date for the introduction of these Scots pines to Muckross is considered to be c.1807 and since the tree *Rhododendron arboreum* was introduced to Britain in 1810 it is possible these two grew up together to form an inspired piece of landscape gardening. It is interesting to note that new plants are being introduced in well-chosen sites to maintain and improve this display in the years to come.

At the lower extremity of this expansive lawn, before turning left to explore the innermost path, the view across the lake should not be missed where in the north-west corner the minute tree-covered speck of Devil's Island invites exploration. Later a stroll around the lakeside can be undertaken by following the pinpointed trails known as Arthur Young's Walk and Mossy Woods Trail. This latter will lead to the largest stand of the indigenous strawberry tree *Arbutus unedo* contained in Killarney. This, the only species of the genus to be found in Western Europe, is only found wild in Cork, Kerry and Sligo in the entire British Isles, the main concentration being centred on the Killarney district. Its main habitat is Mediterranean scrubland, but it also reappears in Portugal, and Brittany in Northern France. There are more alluring prospects along the woodland path, where there beckons a fine specimen of that delicately fern-like foliaged *Chamaecyparis formosensis*, a tender conifer from Taiwan where trees of 200 feet are on record. A close neighbour to this conifer is the very interesting *Chamaecyparis lawsoniana* "Headfort". This rather obscure conifer was raised at the famous Headfort arbotetum near Kells in County Meath, where a specimen has reached 48 feet. Its foliage is blue-grey with silvery white undersides.

From Asia comes another collector's item, *Daphniphyllum macropodum*, a large lustrous leaved evergreen resembling a rhododendron but with scented insignificant-sized flowers. Proof of that temperature comparability with Garinish Island is furnished by the presence here of a stately specimen of the tree fern *Dicksonia antarctica*, with a planting date of 1916.

The adjoining woodland garden probably began its annexation to the lawn area as a woodland walk; now under the protection of a high wire mesh fence, to repel the deer, the open glades have been planted with a collection of plants of particular merit. The opportunity has been seized to assemble a large collection of *Camellia* species and hybrids in a setting ideally suited to the requirements of these most exotic members of the floral scenery.

In this light shade the delicate leaf variegation of *Pittosporum tenuifolium* "Garnettii" is shown to good effect and will undoubtedly prove popular with flower arrangers. That regal *Magnolia* X *soulangiana* "Brozzonii" carries the largest flowers of this group against a background of majestic leaves. A close relation of the camellias on display here is *Stuartia pseudocamellia*, a Japanese plant of real hardiness with single white flowers set with yellow anthers. It can also provide good crimson autumn colour. For those who enjoy golden conifers the *Cedrus deodara* "Aurea" offers a part-time attraction since the golden shading tends to disappear as the season advances.

A plant of much higher merit and some rarity, the Australian *Atherosperma moschatum* is distinguished by its lanceolate leaves with white undersides and creamy-white flowers possessing a compelling fragrance. A fascination for contorted plants seems universal and here *Prunus laurocerasus* "Camelliifolia" provides that interest, its ovate leaves so twisted and contorted that the shrub looks as if it was suffering acute agony.

For autumn colour *Malus sargentii* gives a spectacular display of bright cherry red fruits. The shade tolerant *Stachyurus* is represented here by the Japanese *S. praecox* which opens its long racemes of pale yellow flowers in early spring. This woodland is well suited to the needs of the mahonias which may be seen in several locations. The Himalayan *M. napaulensis* makes a neat well-furnished shrub, flowering in late winter and early spring.

Eucalyptus niphophila also merits a mention, being a tree that should command considerable interest in colder gardens than this. Many authorities regard it as a sub-species of *E. pauciflora*, often being found as a companion to the latter but growing at higher levels. It never attains a large size, tending to be bushy and often distorted, but its bark is cast in a pleasing snake-like pattern of cream interwoven with green and grey.

Future developments are in evidence in a 12-acre paddock on the rising ground above this woodland glade. Here the boundaries have been heavily planted with shelter belt timber since 1973 which is now becoming nicely established. A further matrix of commercial pines and spruces fills the interior at extended distances to permit interplanting of rarer species to proceed. Already some *Acer* have been planted and are becoming established. Perhaps some of the rarer conifers which are limited in their representation here at present will be added to these.

Returning towards the house some splendid groupings of azaleas are very much in evidence. A great clump of *R.* "Amoena" presents a solid mass of magenta-purple bloom. Towards the right the old walled garden has been converted into a propagating area with a large range of greenhouses from which the decorative plants required in the house can always be supplied. This garden will provide the most retentive memory visitors to Killarney will carry back home with them. May they also carry the urge to attempt to grow some of the magnificent plants they have been privileged to view here.

Japanese Gardens

County Kildare

Japanese Gardens, Tully, Co Kildare
Telephone: 045 / 21617

From Dublin take the main road for Cark as far as Kildare Town. Follow the signposts in the town centre for the gardens which are one mile (1.5 Km) south east of the town.

The gardens attached to the National Stud at Tully, Co. Kildare, are unique in being the only authentic Japanese garden in Ireland. They were devised in 1904 by Colonel Hall-Walker, a rather eccentric millionaire who dabbled in things oriental and occult and established Tully as an outstanding stud farm, though even here his fanciful beliefs demanded the immediate sale of any foal born under an inauspicious star.

In 1915 he donated this stud and garden to the British Government in whose possession it remained even after the new Irish State came into being, and was only delivered into the hands of the Irish Government in 1943. It is intriguing to surmise what prompted such a sudden decision in the middle of Britain's preoccupation with World War II.

Once the decision was taken to set up a Japanese garden the Colonel engaged a Japanese father and son, Eida and Minoru, to lay out this unique garden. Their work is regarded as being inferior only to the Emperor's own garden, which their religious cult demanded could never be copied or excelled.

The story this garden attempts to portray—and some theme is woven into most Japenese gardens—is the story of a man making his journey through life, meeting up with his future wife *en route* and thenceforth travelling with her towards their final eternity. The usual vicissitudes of life are represented in this tortuous journey where quarrels and despair give way to moments of supreme elation.

Authenticity has been a keynote of this whole concept and no effort has been spared to create a genuine portrayal of the best of Japanese gardening art. All the objects along the way are of Japanese origin, even the stones of the village having been specially obtained from a Japanese source.

The trees and plants used here, unlike those in many so-called Japanese gardens, are almost exclusively indigenous to Japan. There are a few exceptions, such as the Scots pines dotted around the garden. At the time of construction Japanese pines of this size were not available in Ireland so the best substitute was used and these trees, then well advanced towards maturity, were moved from the adjoining Kildare bogland by Eida and his team of local workmen. Today they and some of the larger trees are causing problems by running short of nourishment, having extracted much of the available food supply in this closely planted confine, which now makes the use of some form of artificial feeding a necessity.

Other traces of European influence introduced after the original construction period are being gradually phased out. One of these not marked for removal is the large blue cedar planted on The Hill of Repose at the end of the open lawn, and which may have been planted to commemorate Eida after his death in London in 1912.

The Tea House, an integral part of Japanese gardens, built completely of teak and roofed with teak shingles (thatch was the original roof material) constitutes the focal point of the garden, and is surrounded by some outstanding examples of the Bonsai art. One larch is of very great antiquity and may have been a companion of the one to be seen beside the Italian garden pool at Garinish Island.

The miniature village to be seen facing the Tea House shows some remarkable carved stone containers in which Bonsai plants are growing. The range of trees used is very wide indeed revealing a preference for the conifers which include junipers, cedar, *Cryptomeria*, yew and others. The broad leaved trees are also represented with birch and maple perhaps the favourites, but I also noticed a whole clump of Bonsai beech set in a stone container.

Perhaps less easy to comprehend is the rock and sand garden of more recent construction which is to be seen in the plot of ground to the rear of the big blue cedar. Were it not for the descriptive plaque one might conjecture for a considerable time the possible meaning of this bizarre arrangement. The title given to it is "The Garden of Eternity". It is a design on the Karesansui style associated with the Zen monks who exerted a dominant influence stretching from the 12th to the 15th centuries. The Zen sect originally came from China bringing with them a new culture with a contemplative foundation linking it to garden creation.

The rocks that figure in this large bed of sand are symbolic of good and evil urges while the tree *Cercidiphyllum japonicum*, with leaves rather similar to the Judas tree, represents a transformation from depravity. In contrast to the other garden this is purely spiritual and might be better regarded as a form of surrealist imagism depicting spiritual mutations. For those versed in Japanese culture and history this may represent a very fascinating addition to the gardens.

These gardens provide an opportunity to view a collection of the principal trees and plants of Japan. What a pity those scots pines could not be changed for *Pinus densiflora*, in some ways the Japanese equivalent of *P. sylvestris*; the Japanese picture would then be nearly complete. With such a wealth of other beautiful trees around the garden, it brings a realisation of what a rich flora this highly industrialised country possesses.

Once inside, the scene changes to walks lined with acers and overhead a graceful *Cryptomeria japonica*. It is interesting to note the habit this tree has of forming cones on the tips of its branches which then grow through the cone. The acers, at all times graceful trees, don the most alluring autumn colours, making this garden a place of exquisite beauty in the days approaching winter.

Even come winter the coral bark maple, *Acer palmatum* "Senkaki", is still a charming sight with the coral red of its young branches, having earlier displayed its canary-yellow autumn leaves. Perhaps the most beautiful of all the Japanese maples is that with the tongue twisting name of *Acer palmatum* var. *heptalobum* "Osakazuki", its green leaves turning a fiery scarlet in autumn.

Besides its maples the garden contains many other

interesting shrubs of Japanese origin. In Japan, paper is made from the paper mulberry, *Broussonetia papyrifera*, and this tree can be seen around the dark tunnel. Nearby a dwarf sized, perhaps Bonsaied *Hamamelis japonica* flowers in early spring carrying wispy yellow flowers, and also provides pleasing autumn colour prolonged in some cases by its habit of leaf retention.

The presence of *Decaisnea fargesii* is rather unexpected since most would regard this as a Chinese shrub and the same comment might be passed on *Koelreuteria paniculata*. No such criticism can be levelled against the elegant *Hydrangea paniculata* "Grandiflora", a white free-flowering variety of considerable distinction.

One plant that typifies Japan is the sacred bamboo *Nandina domestica*, and here there is one fine example, with panicles of white flowers in late summer, and coral red leaves. Strangely enough this is the only example of the sacred bamboo to be found in the gardens. Of the conifers the umbrella pine, *Sciadopitys verticillata*, is certainly indigenous to Japan but is now restricted to two small areas.

Water is a feature throughout this garden, sometimes channelled into narrow, shallow streams then expanding into quite sizeable riverlets or trapped in placid back waters, but always crystal clear, symbolic in its movement of this story of a life told in stones, trees and water.

In an adjoining enclosure, a small lake in a more conventional setting lifts the spell of Japanese influence. Here a long hedge of copper beech lines the sidewalk, looking very decorative with hues of varying shades resulting from its regulated clippings. Some huge clumps of *Gunnera* are planted along the damp margins of the lakeside. A young *Metasequoia glyptostroboides* of about 10 years is making very rapid growth in this cool damp soil, as are a line of magnolias of similar age. These will make a very attractive feature of this satellite garden, further enhanced by a collection of rhododendrons.

Fittingly the visit concludes with a look at the garden centre sales area, where a very fair collection of plants is presented. In the adjoining heated conservatory, where indoor plants and literature on the garden are on sale, the walls are adorned with flowering and foliage plants, including a passion flower climbing over a lattice wood ceiling with its fruits temptingly suspended. An unusual feature of this centre is the small passageway in which small Bonsai subjects are offered for sale. These would provide an interesting memento of a visit to this most exceptional garden.

Emo Court

County Laois

Emo Court, Emo, Co Laois
Telephone: 0502 / 26110

These gardens are situated just over a mile (2 Km) off the main
Cork road 45 miles (75 Km) south west of Dublin.

Emo is large and scattered, occupying an area of 85 acres, approximately 35 hectares. This area includes a large picturesque lake, its waters on one bank overhung by many beautiful trees. It is also a young garden in the sense that it has been recreated by its present owner Mr C D Cholmeley-Harrison, whose purchase of the property at a time when it had fallen into complete decay has resulted not alone in the arresting of its decline, but in the creation of a garden richer in every way than at any period in its past history.

Emo Court was formerly owned by the Earls of Portarlington. It passed out of the possession of this family in 1920, after which it stood empty for 10 years before being acquired by a religious order which did little to preserve and much to desecrate its beauty. When purchased in 1969 by its present owner it bore little resemblance to Gandon's masterpiece of 1790.

A very considerable sum of money went into its restoration, involving the renewal of large portions of its interior and ornate ceiling work; a job carried out in most masterly fashion by a team of local craftsmen. Of the estate, 250 acres were bought by Mr Cholmeley-Harrison, much of the remaining 14,000 acres being acquired by the Department of Forestry.

Fortunately fine mature timber can withstand years of neglect and Emo possesses many stately trees, probably planted around the mid-nineteenth century. Within this framework, a garden of new plantings was created, ranging from a wide and selective collection of rhododendrons and camellias to some of the most decorative of the conifers. Moreover, new

117

clearings are being made of old game cover to extend the area covered by exotic trees and shrubs.

The imprint of the Portarlington period of residence may still be seen in the mile long avenue of redwoods, *Sequoiadendron giganteum*, planted in 1853. Only a portion of this planting lies within the boundary of the present Emo Court estate, the remainder being owned by the Department of Forestry. The tallest tree in this avenue had reached 118 feet when measurements were last taken.

There are also some other significant trees remaining from this earlier stewardship. These include a *Pinus radiata* of 98 feet, a *Picea smithiana* of 88 feet, a solitary *Cupressus macrocarpa*, the lone survivor of a wind blown clump, the highest of which measured 97 feet, and lastly a very fine *Cedrus deodara* of 97 feet.

The remaining plantings of this earlier period include two very large *Kalmia*, one of which has become over-shaded and flowers sparsely. The new plantings, which extend over a very considerable area, have all been carried out over the past 12 years. These include a scattering of rhododendrons, most of medium size with a few of the tree-size types, but lacking the very attractive and accommodating dwarfs. One interesting claret-red hybrid with dark markings and distinctive coppery foliage looks good in the woodland setting. It is unnamed but its late June flowering and other characteristics suggest that one parent might be *R. griersonianum*. There is also a good plant of that exquisite blue *R. augustinii*, its sky blue shade lighting up the woodland glade. The owner is fortunate in having a soil to suit these fastidious plants, and is taking full advantage of his good fortune by using the woodland sites to house a fairly comprehensive collection of carefully selected plants which provide so much colour for so many months of the year.

A collection of camellias, while much less extensive, is still large enough to become a showpiece of this garden. They occupy a site to the left of the pathway leading to the lake. The position is again light woodland with just the right degree of shade for these sun-hating plants. Planted against a north-facing wall they will thrive, but given a south wall site they will quickly die.

It is difficult to understand why a greater use of camellias is not a feature of Irish gardens. These superb plants are perfectly hardy and much less demanding in their soil requirements than are rhododendrons. This planting may require a few years before becoming an outstanding feature of this garden, but as they are early flowerers, an improved showing may be expected as each year passes. Spring time is the showiest season in most gardens, but here, where there is not formality but just natural light woodland planted with these colourful shades, it is the period when this garden reaches perfection.

A supporting show of other shrubs certainly exists but still lacks maturity although improving with the passing of every year. Such items as a snowdrop tree, *Halesia carolina*, carrying white snowdrop-like flowers, is a rapid grower and early to flower while still uncommon enough to be an unusual attraction.

The *Cornus* chosen here is *C. nuttallii* which forms a magnificent small tree but takes its time in doing so and can be tender in its early stages. The floral bracts appearing in late May are pure white but show pink tinges as they age. Several conifers have also been planted, including the not too often featured *Torreya californica*, both hardy and very handsome with masses of dark green large leaved foliage.

The lake, covering an area of around 20 acres, provides an all-season appeal. The path along the near bank affords continuous viewing of the timber-clad opposite shore where the trees set very close to the edge cast shadows across the water. Lofty Scots pines display their straight russet brown trunks with the soft greens of the neighbouring beeches giving colour contrasts. In autumn all is lit up with the many coloured hues silhouetted against the water.

An assortment of bird life is another of the lake's attractions with stately swans gliding between their feeding grounds and moorhens scuttling through the aquatic vegetation around the water edges. By good fortune lonely herons may occasionally be sighted prospecting their fishing grounds or standing long-legged, motionless in the shallows, waiting for their prey.

The planting along the lake-side walk will eventually make a very considerable contribution to the interest and beauty of this area. Additional autumn colour is provided by a *Fothergilla major,* a shrub with small ivory white flowers, but more distinguished by its rich claret colouring before leaf fall. Another contribution is the even more colourful *Parrotia persica,* a native of Persia, with a warm autumn colour blend of amber and scarlet, so pleasing in the rather cheerless days of October. This shrub is very lime tolerant. These and the white flowering eucryphias prolong the viewing season into the days of autumn. The earlier season in this part of the garden is brightened by the viburnums, the multi-coloured azaleas and other members of the heather family.

Various new plantings have been dotted round the large parkland area, already furnished with some good specimens of mature timber. Additions include the beautiful *Abies delavayi* var. *forrestii* and the coast redwood, *Sequoia sempervirens.* *Eucalyptus* are being attempted in this midland garden and already some measure of success has been achieved with *E. gunnii* now of flowering size. The hardiness of *E. gunnii* may perhaps be attributed to the fact that seed is being distributed from trees growing in the coldest areas of these islands, where it has been acclimatised to everything our winters can offer. Others on trial here are *E. tasmanica* and *E. coccifera.*

New beds of *Kalmia latifolia* are growing well, their pale pink campanulate flowers arriving at the end of the rhododendron season. Another planting which will later provide spectacular colour is the handkerchief or dove tree, *Davidia involucrata,* discovered by Pere David, the French missionary plant hunter.

Visitors to this garden may find late spring or early summer the best periods for viewing; at this time the rhododendrons and camellias will be at their peak, but autumn can often be spectacular with many good colour subjects.The latest project at Emo, commenced in the autumn of 1984, has been the development of an old disused drive known as Mad Margaret's

Walk. Here large areas of laurel have been cut away and uprooted, the better to display the stems of fine native timber lining the driveway, and to provide a protective setting for the planting of shade-bearing plants of botanical interest and also to introduce a more colourful scenic effect.

Birr Castle

County Offaly

Birr Castle, Birr, Co Offaly
Telephone: 0509 / 20056

Birr is situated 88 miles (143 Km) east of Dublin and is easily
accessible from the towns of Athlone, Tullamore and Roscrea.
The castle is well signposted and just a few minutes walk from
the town centre.

Birr Castle and its gardens nestle against the western perimeter of the town of Birr. The approach to the castle gates is down a wide chestnut-lined spur road from the main street, where adequate parking facilities are available for both cars and buses. No cars are permitted entry to the castle grounds. Opposite the entrance visitors can obtain luncheons and teas in the garden restaurant, beside which is situated the Tourist Office. The former is open from April to October.

The gardens cover 62 hectares and for a reasonably full viewing around four hours would be required. Seats and tables have been provided at strategic viewing points around the walks.

Throughout their existence the gardens have been supportive of plant collecting expeditions, thereby ensuring a continuous supply of new material for propagation. The more recent expeditions with which Birr has been associated have been those of Roy Lancaster and, as late as 1986, the Keith Rushforth expedition. In 1984 Lord Rosse himself participated in an expedition to Nepal. Birr is one of the very few gardens where a full time propagator is employed. Plant material so raised is available for exchange with other major gardens and botanical institutions as well as being sold to visitors at the castle entrance.

Inside the castle gates is a vast and very beautiful piece of parkland dotted with specimens of fine timber, beneath many of which have been planted rings of daffodils, these being rotationally dug up, thinned and re-planted. In the centre of this park a specimen of the rather rare lime *Tilia chingiana* was planted in 1946. This tree has now attained a height of 35 feet. The gardens contain a very good representation of the less usual *Tilia* including *T.* "Moltkei", *T. chinensis, T. dasystyla, T. henryana* and several of the common lines *T.* X *europaea.*

At the junction where the entrance road meets that surrounding the park there is a small bed containing just one tree. This is *Euodia daniellii* planted as a memorial to the gardens' principal architect, the sixth Earl. It produces white flowers in late summer. Around this centrepiece is a surround of the carpeting *Omphalodes cappadocica,* popularly known as blue eyed mary.

To the right lies the Picnic and Playground area which also contains some interesting trees. The *Lonicera* near the entrance is a hybrid named *L.* "Michael Rosse" obtained by the present Earl's grandfather from a crossing of an unknown parent with *L. etrusca.* This plant received an RHS Award of Merit. Nearby can be seen the slow growing kermes oak, *Quercus coccifera.* This is the host plant of the Kermes insect from which the dye cochineal is obtained. Its neighbour is another little known oak recorded as *Q. macrolepis* and distinguished by its chrys-antheum-like fruits. A rather singular juniper, *Juniperus deppeana* var. *pachyphlaea* has flaky bark patterned like a crocodile skin. This is a tree said to be very difficult to establish. Here also is a specimen of the very graceful *Cedrus deodara* whose shoot extremities droop to create a slightly weeping effect.

Approaching the Formal Garden a *Magnolia* "Elizabeth" may attract some attention. This yellow flowered *Magnolia* was raised in Brooklyn Botanic Garden, USA, and is a cross between *M. acuminata* and *M. hypoleuca.* Here also on view are *Koelreutia paniculata* and its variety *apiculata.* These Chinese trees carry small yellow flowers in panicles sufficent-ly massed to be quite effective. In any case the large pinnate leaves are a feature in themselves.

Inside this enclosed garden the design belongs to a past age when staff were plentiful and cheap. An elaborate series of hornbeam *allées* criss-crosses the garden creating shady 10-feet-high tunnel walks with wide spacings to admit the entry of sunlight. Necklaces of snowdrops line the base of the trees providing a late winter attraction. In addition, a boxwood *parterre* follows an intricately woven pattern to produce, at intervals, boxes in which individual lilacs have been planted.

Against the west facing wall has been planted the *Paeonia* "Anne Rosse", a hybrid raised by the Earl of Rosse in 1950. In front of this stands an ornamental white seat made by the estate carpenter from Birr oak, with a scroll back design carrying the letters M.R. (Michael Rosse, Sixth Earl). Facing this at the opposite end of the walk is a matching seat designed with crossed Rs.

Flanked by the range of hothouses now used for propagating, there stands a pillared colonnade over which clambers a large *Wisteria*. In the same area may be seen a magnificent *Magnolia stellata* which has grown far beyond its normal span and must be the largest plant of its kind to be seen in this country. To its right a Japanese bitter orange tree, *Poncirus trifoliata*, fills the air with the scent of its white blooms in May.

Below the houses four Chinese *Ginkgo* trees are making steady growth for an area so vulnerable to frost. At the opposite end of the houses should be noted a large *Sequoiadendron giganteum* with a planting date of circa 1855, and a height recording of 76 feet. Its neighbour *Cedrela sinensis* at 60 feet is equally impressive with large pinnate leaves and trusses of white flowers in late summer.

Glancing towards the kitchen garden on the right brings into view a quite remarkable narrow avenue of boxwood hedges some thirty feet tall and planted around 300 years ago. Beyond these are a clump of some of the original *Paeonia* "Anne Rosse" hybrid, which resulted from a crossing of *P. delavayi* with *P. lutea*. The large flowers are yellow with a centre of red stamens and crimson streakings on the reverse.

On leaving the walled garden through the little gothic side gate there is a large *Staphylea holocarpa* carrying long racemes of white flowers in early summer. Camellias are in evidence against the wall on the left, though for these the natural soil here is not suitable. Further along may be noted a well developed *Torreya californica*, a conifer of good quality, well furnished with large dark green shining foliage. Nearby the very unusual *Eucommia ulmoides* is distinguished by its curious leaves from which rubber may be obtained. These if gently torn in two halves will continue to hang together, still joined by invisible strands of latex.

Across the road a sign signals the way to the Fernery. Firstly there may be seen another plant with family connections, *Berberis* X *lologensis* "Nymans". This carries yellow flowers with red inside petals. This may in fact be the only plant in existence since none remain at Nymans. Here also is the Chinese ash, *Fraxinus chinensis,* mainly characterised by its wine-purple autumn colour.

The Fernery has been newly excavated from a slow flowing stream choked with years of leaf and silt deposits. Now it maintains a uniform level at the bottom of two inclining banks most suitable for all types of fern. As yet only *Polystichum setiferum* and *Phyllitis scolopendrium* are in evidence, but, given the indefatigable energy of Lord Rosse, many more will very shortly follow. Another feature has been the dam erected to create a miniature waterfall on another portion of stream, beneath which has been unearthed an old fountain now restored to functioning condition.

On the adjoining island, called Inisdara, stand two particularly fine trees. *Pseudotsuga menziesii* when measured in 1966 by Lanning Roper stood at 115 feet. This tree comes from western North America, but a little distance away grows a splendid native, *Quercus robur*. This is the oak most frequently met with in the rich lowland soils while *Q. petraea* is the upland tree of more acidic soils. Large tracts of the latter tree are to be found in the Killarney National Park, but do not feature at Birr.

A short distance from the island exit bridge is *Populus lasiocarpa*, one of the most decorative poplars. The leaves especially on young trees can be very large indeed and are carried on bright red petioles. On the other side of the walk is a group of three *Larix kaempferi*. This Japanese larch is decorative both in spring , with its delicate green foliage and red flowers, and in autumn when its colour can be a rich gold.

The river Brosna is now crossed by a brick bridge. This

divides that part of the garden in County Tipperary from the major portion in County Offaly. On the right of the bridge is a rustic table and seats from which a fine view of the Castle may be obtained. There are ten of these seating units scattered through the gardens, mostly placed to provide strategic viewing points.

Facing the bridge is one of the most imaginative pieces of planting I have seen for a long time. Here has been put down an avenue of *Prunus* "Accolade." Unfortunately the parents of this hybrid are not known for certain; speculation favours *P. sargentii* and *P. subhirtella* as being the most probable. This cherry was raised at the Knap Hill Nursery in 1938, and received an Award of Merit in 1961. Unlike so many *Prunus* there is neither overcrowding of flowers or branches. It forms an open spreading tree with attractive winter tracery. The deep rosy pink semi-double flowers are large and appear either solitary or in umbels of three. Compared to other cherries this variety is scantily clad, giving better effect to its individual flowers and creating a very graceful effect. The trees, obtained from Hilliers, were a present from the Dowager Lady Rosse. I echo her choice.

The surrounding area, known as the Arboretum, contains many trees of distinction. Away to the right where scrub has been cleared a young collection of limes has been set out. These include *Tilia henryana* and *T. chingiana*. The oriental beech *Fagus orientalis* might well be mistaken for the ordinary beech but provides richer autumn colour.

Conifers abound here, none more distinguished than *Picea likiangensis*, a native of Western China and Tibet. In mid-May this tree is adorned with masses of crimson male flowers and bright red females; the young cones are also reddish pink. *Picea spinulosa*, belonging to the flat leaved group of spruces, is somewhat similar to *P. smithiana*, but is only pendulous in its branch ends whereas the latter is also pendulous in its branchlets and has quadrangular leaves. Both grow here in close proximity affording an excellent opportunity for comparison. Variety is provided by the deciduous *Larix laricina*, a native of North America and not entirely at home in these climates. It may be distinguished by its small neat cones. Also represented here are the *forrestii* and *georgei* varieties of *Abies delavayi*. Both are equally good, making decorative shapely trees with prominent white bands of stomata on the lower leaf surfaces and large deep purple barrel-shaped cones. The *Metasequoia glyptostroboides* is one of the original specimens distributed from Kew and was planted in the very early fifties.

Close to the bridge leaving the Arboretum grows an evergreen oak, *Quercus wislizenii*, with holly-like leaves. This Californian tree is somewhat rare, perhaps because of its slow growth rate and rather shrub-like appearance.

The walk proceeding towards the castle along the bank of the river Camcor reveals considerable clearance operations along the far bank. These have exposed a stand of Serbian spruce, *Picea omorika*, a tree of spire-like habit with an individual quality of distinction. It can be stated without question that this is the most decorative of all European conifers.

Near to the old boathouse can be seen a weeping beech, *Fagus sylvatica* "Pendula". It is not an unusual tree but this in no way detracts from its very evident charm. Close by grows *Cornus nuttallii*, one of the more sought-after dogwoods. Under favourable conditions it may reach tree size, but it does prefer an acid soil. The autumn colour is sometimes red and the bracts borne in May are an ivory white becoming pink.

Past the boat house the lower walk takes in the River Garden and embraces a rich area of important plantings on both sides of the river. A giant *Populus canescens* 108 feet high dominates the scene and bears comparison with any of its kind in the British Isles. Closer to the river the cork oak *Quercus suber* makes a small tree quite unlike the commercial specimens to be seen in the Iberian Peninsula and in parts of South America.

In this garden heartland are to be found some of Birr's outstanding plants. Here the columnar 35-foot-tall *Eucryphia nymansensis* "Nymansay" has an abundance of white flowers two inches in diameter carried from August to September. This variety is named after the garden of Nymans, home of Anne, Countess of Rosse. Another good plant is the incense-scented *Magnolia officinalis*, flowering in June and making a stately tree of around 40 feet. Further down on the opposite bank *Magnolia dawsoniana* makes an even more magnificent plant. The leaves, some six inches long, clothe the tree after its large, March-opening, pale-rose flowers have departed. Alongside on the far river bank the very rare *Carrierea calycina*, planted by the present Earl's grandfather, has creamy-white candelabra-like racemes of flowers in late June.

Another *Magnolia* with family associations, *Magnolia* X *loebneri* "Leonard Messel", was raised at Nymans by the Dowager Lady Rosse's father, Colonel Messel. The flowers are purplish pink on the outside and white within. The cross is thought to be between *M. kobus* and *M. stellata* forma *rosea*. Yet another magnolia indicating the quality and depth of this collection cannot be passed without mention. Again on the distant bank, *Magnolia* X *veitchii* flowers in April. This is a hybrid between the famous *M. campbellii* and *M. denudata*; of the five plants resulting from the cross only one had pink blossoms, to which the name *veitchii* was given. The flowers open in April, before the foot long leaves which follow. Finally, on the castle terrace and enjoying the shelter of the wall, a 20 foot tall *Magnolia delavayi* has now regained full vigour after a severe set back from the frost of 1979. The flowers, 7 to 8 inches across, are creamy-white and fragrant but rather short lived.

The river below the castle is spanned by a suspension bridge built about 1815, but not now open to the public. Just above the bridge a steep embankment sweeps down to the water's edge. Near the top of this embankment new plantings are being attempted; foremost among these are some *Edgeworthia chrysantha* (Syn. *E. papyrifera*). This deciduous Chinese shrub produces slightly fragrant yellow flowers in terminal clusters. A high class paper for use in making currency has been produced from this plant in Japan. It is only marginally hardy, having failed at Kew.

A return to the high walk leading back towards the boathouse can be profitably undertaken. Here at the outset a *Cedrus atlantica* forma *glauca* is on view. This most popular cedar is valued for its bluish tints, deeper on some trees than others, but attractive in all its forms. Further along a 40-foot *Ehretia dicksonii* produces fragrant white flowers in late summer. Below the path a large plane *Platanus acerifolia*, a tree of great vigour and long life span, has not yet reached full size.

Below this walk two very renowned magnolias dominate the scene. *Magnolia campbellii* planted here in 1949 appears in few gardens, not because of any lack of appreciation of its unquestionable beauty, but owing to a lack of confidence in many gardeners that they will survive the 40-year span before this tree will produce its first flowers. Of similar status but earlier to flower is the strong growing *M. campbellii* "Charles Raffill", a cross made by Charles Raffill of Kew between the type and var. *mollicomata* which was first distributed in 1948. The very large flowers are deep rose-pink when in bud opening to rose-purple on the outside and white inside.

While full mention has been made of the very representative *Magnolia* presence in this garden, the acers which also figure strongly here have been largely ignored. Acers are scattered over a wide area of the gardens and include *A. triflorum*, brilliant in its autumn colour; *A. griseum*, the acer for all seasons with its winter bark attraction; *A. rufinerve* providing snake bark effects; *A. oliverianum*, *A. cappadocicum*, *A. ginnala*, *A. nikoense* and many others.

Finally it is only a short way from this high walk across the park to the famous telescope, passing on the way the Lilac walk where in season one can enjoy the colour and scent these plants provide. Lilacs at Birr include *Syringa villosa*, *S.* X *josiflexa*, *S. pinnatifolia* and *S. sweginzowii*.

The plant content of this garden has over the years been fully documented with a meticulous recording of the positional planting of all trees and shrubs by Michael Rosse, the Sixth Earl. Modern methods have now taken over but the painstaking work of former owners still remains the solid foundation on which the history of every tree at Birr can be determined.

Belvedere

County Westmeath

Belvedere, Mullingar, Co Westmeath
Telephone: Information from Westmeath County Council at
044 / 40861

Mullingar is 51 miles (83 Km) from Dublin along well signposted main roads. The gardens are situated 4 miles (6.5 Km) south of Mullingar, between Lough Ennel and the road to Tullamore.

Oh gay lapped the waves on the shores of Lough Ennell
And sweet smelt the breeze amid the garlic and fennel
But sweeter and gayer than either of these
Were the songs of the birds in Lord Belvedere's trees

These lines penned by John Betjeman on the occasion of a lakeside grotto picnic carry a picture of a gay social event, but with an underlying note of bodement. Such was the atmosphere that invaded this mini mansion on the shore of Lough Ennell from the very beginning of the occupancy of its owner, Baron Robert Belfield, later Lord Belvedere, in the mid eighteenth century.

A few years earlier this cavalier socialite had married the 16-year-old daughter of Viscount Molesworth, but during his lengthy absences from Gaulstown, the family home, she sought the company of Robert's brother Arthur, a close neighbour. Robert, convinced that intimacy had taken place between them, set up house in Belvedere and had his wife imprisoned at Gaulstown six miles distant. Here for 31 years she was to watch her youth drain away while reflecting on the cruel ethos of high society.

Meanwhile, Robert became envious of the rising fortunes of his brother George, who half a mile away on the eastern shore of Lough Ennell had build himself the very imposing Rochford House, later named Tudenham. This envy culminated in a fit of infatuated fury in which he decided to erect a building that would cut out the distasteful view of his brother's opulence. In 1755 the gothic castellated folly later to

135

become known as The Jealous Wall was erected. The architect responsible for this remarkable folly is thought by some to have been the Florentine Barradotte, while others ascribe it to Thomas Wright of Durham, who is known to have executed similar works in Ireland.

In 1744 Robert died and was succeeded in the title by his son George Augustus the 2nd Earl, who embarked on the building of a town house in keeping with his station. Belvedere House in Great Denmark Street, Dublin was completed in 1786 and today, still maintaining its original magnificence, it houses one of the city's leading schools, Belvedere College.

The second Earl died without an heir and the property passed to a series of owners over the next 100 years, finally descending to Charles Marley, who added the stylish terraces facing the lake and began the development of the present day picturesque walled garden. This was further improved by his cousin Col. Howard Bury, who in his army wanderings learned the art of plant collecting. His additions to the gardens were many. Within the walled garden he had several glasshouses erected and outside he engaged in a wide variety of plantings, many of which still exist today.

When in the 1960s Col. Howard Bury died, the estate passed to his close friend Rex Beaumont who, like the Colonel, was a keen plantsman and shared the garden with the public by staging open days. In 1982 Belvedere passed out of private ownership, being purchased by the Westmeath County Council for a sum of £250,000. This would appear a very sound investment made at a time when land values were depressed, and when it is considered that the property contains an 18 hole golf course in splendid condition. Westmeath has therefore become the first rural county council to own and maintain a period mansion and historic garden of high potential for public access.

Belvedere, with its flamboyant history, is a subject of widespread interest and the decision of Westmeath County Council to restore this garden and open it to the public will give satisfaction to all concerned about its future. The Jealous Wall, for example, is a reminder of the autocratic whims which held sway in the social life of the eighteenth century. There is today more than ever before a fascination in such aspects of history, and most would mourn their disappearance.

Others too must have a feeling for Belvedere. The fact that this remote lakeside villa fathered one of Dublin's most distinguished town houses can hardly escape historical notice by those whose education has been received at Belvedere College, and also by those who govern the destinies of that great college. They too must be watching with considerable interest the planning of Westmeath County Council with regard to the future of Belvedere. It is known that James Joyce had contemplated writing a book on the history of Belvedere but abandoned the idea when he discovered that the Countess of Belvedere had never been permited to live there.

The gardens of Belvedere prior to their rebirth have been the subject of much nostalgic affection, some no doubt deserved, some exaggerated. Great gardeners and plantsmen have worked here and some of the fruits of their labours still survive, but much has vanished. The work of restoration has begun but time must elapse before some of the newer plantings acquire the charm and character of established plants.

The garden might be divided into two parts consisting of the walled garden and the arboretum surrounding the house. The walled garden is quite different in character from the typical enclosed garden which was usually laid out in a geometric square and devoted to the growing of vegetables and cut flowers for the house. The most striking aspect of this Belvedere garden is its unusual narrow rectangular shape which on entering permits a panoramic view of its colourful interior. The area of 1.5 acres is packed with plants, with a small lawn space set with rose beds. It still retains all the hallmarks associated with an 18th century pleasure garden.

When Col. Howard Bury developed this garden he brought to it the choice flowering plants he had encountered in his journeys. Many still grow here, like the gentian-blue *Echinops*, over which the butterflies dance a ballet as the bees seek the nectar. That old eighteenth century introduction, *Fothergilla major*, has blooms like a demure bottlebrush. The presence of this acid-liking shrub surely makes the growing of some rhododendrons a possibility.

This is a garden for old roses and they are well represented, bringing as always an allurement of delicate colour and intimate scent. There are also some superb *Hydrangea*, both species and cultivars. Here is a garden fashioned in a different century and as such possessing distinctive charms not always to be found in more modern gardens. Most of these plants can probably be attributed to Col. Bury, including the *Decaisnea fargesii* in the top right hand corner. This plant, although first introduced in the last century, has only latterly acquired some notice and can still hardly be termed a popular shrub.

Outside the walled garden there are about 12 acres of enclosed grounds containing more of Col. Bury's fancies and perhaps some plantings of his successor, Rex Beaumont, who had a knowledgeable interest in the gardens and opened them to the public on occasions.

The presence of *Metasequoia* here denotes that plantings continued up to the late 1940s, the date of introduction of these trees. A fine *Thuja plicata* introduced nearly a hundred years before the *Metasequoia* still remains one of the most distinguished trees with its coppery red bark. The pendulous *Picea smithiana* also adds distinction to this collection, which, when clearance is completed, may reveal many more noteworthy trees. Westmeath has always enjoyed a reputation for the size and quality of its beech trees and some of them here could rank with the best.

Some trees which have become both old and dangerous may have to be taken out. It is to be hoped that their replacements will be in character with this old garden. New exotic plantings should be avoided. Every other garden in the country has been engaged in planting such trees and their introduction here would gain no particular distinction.

Both house and gardens are open to the public from April to September.

John F. Kennedy Park

County Wexford

John F Kennedy Park, New Ross, Co Wexford
Telephone: 051 / 88171

Drive west from Wexford town for 18 miles (29 Km) to
Ballynabola Cross. Turn left and follow signposts from there.

The John F. Kennedy Arboretum, situated 8 miles south of New Ross and 9 miles from the coast, began its existence in 1964, four years before its official opening. Its first director was the late Mr Tony Hanan, a man of the widest talents who contributed so much to the formative years of this arboretum and to Irish arboriculture in general. The initial plans formulated by Mr Hanan have been faithfully adhered to by succeeding Directors, who have sought to build upon and enlarge the formative design laid down at the inception of the arboretum.

The fact that the arboretum is administered by Coillte Teoranta, the Irish Forestry Board, in co-operation with the Department of Agriculture, gives it an underlying research character. The plant collection here has a scientific aspect, combined with plantings of species plots whose sylvicultural characteristics can be observed and studied. These objectives are blended as far as possible to provide an attractive amenity appearance. Any criticism of Kennedy Arboretum must be weighed against its value as a research institution.

It would be impossible to endow this newcomer with the atmosphere prevailing in older institutions where historical influences play a prominent role. Kennedy was created out of plain fields and will require generations before it acquires that elusive appeal found in places of antiquity.

The setting out of the specimen trees in groups of three while making scientific sense is not the ideal way of presentation to gain full aesthetic value. The fact that 100,000 visitors flock to Kennedy arboretum every year proves its undoubted attractions. This figure compares favourably with the high attendance figures of Nature Parks in Northern Ireland.

The park has a total of 623 acres of which 310 are devoted to the plant collection. It reaches its highest elevation of 890 feet at the summit of Slieve Coillte, which acts as a vantage point for viewing the whole arboretum and much of the countryside beyond. The soil over most of the area consists of a deep loam earth with a pH ranging from 5.4 to 7.0, the former being eminently suitable for the growing of rhododendrons and other ericaceous plants. The area can claim the highest sun duration figure for the entire country, a factor of considerable significance in relation to plant growth. Conifers in particular, which are capable of making growth throughout the entire year would be the main beneficiaries.

The director's office is reminiscent of an operations head-quarters where the exact position of any unit at any particular time can be instantly pinpointed. Name a tree and its location, provided it is contained in the collection, can be pinpointed at a glance through the charts. Furthermore its filing cabinet record will reveal when planting took place, from where it was obtained and its vital statistics at each five year measurement. The task of measuring all the trees and shrubs occupies one month. These at the moment amount to approximately 4,500 species and varieties but full establishment strength aims at a figure of 6,000.

The principal sources from which trees are obtained are commercial nurseries, botanic gardens and other arboreta, in the form of plants or seed. Some difficulty seems to surround supplies from the two areas of eastern North America and China, but in general all arboreta conduct an international seed exchange system.

A broad comparison could be made between this research arboretum and the Forestry Genetic station at Kilmacurragh. The latter's interest is primarily confined to improving the strains of those species already in use in our state forests. Here the emphasis is much more diversified and embraces the study of a much wider range of trees with more consideration being given to their environmental value. An important part of the research being carried out here relates to the experimentation with different elm clones. The need to find an elm with disease resistance is a matter of urgency and widespread international trials are being carried out to find a replacement for our sick elms.

The value placed on the environmental aspect is shown by the departure from taxonomic classification in the tree groupings. To relieve the winter bleakness of massed deciduous species, a system has been devised whereby the Gymnosperms (conifers) although contained in a different circuit are at intervals interwoven with the Angiospermae circuit.

One may have doubts about the environmental character of the main building block. It cannot be said that it is incompatible with its setting because both are modern. Much care went into its construction, the stone having been transported from a quarry in Clare. At the same time some disquiet may be felt about a building manifestly urban set in an arboretum slowly gaining a sylvan atmosphere. The four stone and timber shelters placed at points around the circuit are less conspicious as they are draped with climbing plants, but even here the use of native undressed sculptured oak might have been preferable.

The arboretum is traversed by a two mile long circular road beginning and ending at the reception centre. Motorists are not permitted to use this road. Most visitors should find there are so many interesting trees and shrubs along both sides of the route that the walk will not seem unduly long.

First will be encountered the North West American plots of *Tsuga*, *Sequoiadendron* and *Abies lasiocarpa*, the alpine fir. Here also a plot of *Sequoia sempervirens* are showing their susceptibility to wind damage. Further along on the left the maple cultivars are planted in groups of three of a kind, with a windbreak backing of native hardwoods. Grass around the tree bases is controlled by Roundup.

In complete contrast there follows a rock garden planting of dwarf and slow growing conifers. The area is roughly an acre and has been designed to simulate alpine valleys. The *Picea abies* cultivars include the remarkable "Clanbrassiliana" from Northern Ireland, now a very old discovery, which has withstood all modern challengers. It forms a dense flat-topped mat, much wider than it is high. Another horizontal developer is *Juniperus procumbens* "Nana" which makes a very good ground cover.

In all there are around 300 species and cultivars at present in this collection but the ultimate target is a showing of 400 of these alluring dwarfs. The backing hedge of *Podocarpus andinus*, a native of Chile sometimes referred to as the plum fruited yew, is arresting in its most unusual use as a hedge plant. One of the park's four shelters stands at the southern end of this alpine garden and is partially covered by a rampant wisteria.

The next section is one of the best features of early spring with a large array of *Prunus* providing a tremulous mass of soft colour. On the other side of the avenue other members of the Rosaceae prolong this display of colour.

The small lake of less than an acre is an important feature in adding variety to this flat unrelieved landscape. An island planted with *Gunnera* provides this architectural plant with a fitting setting to display itself to the very best advantage. The marshy edges of this pond provide excellent sites for natural waterside plant life and for introduced water plants.

The half-mile vista stretching from near the perimeter to the reception centre was an inspired piece of planting. Landscapes through the centuries have favoured both straight and curved regimented avenues. Here a new concept of total informality is employed, which, when a state of maturity is reached, will carry views of fine timber in an assortment of shapes and sizes.

Other attempts at relief landscaping include mixing the evergreen X *Cupressocyparis leylandii* with *Sorbus* to produce a winter appeal. Unfortunately the close planting will diminish the individual characteristic of many trees, although this will be mitigated by later removals. This is inevitable when research is the primary object. Here if you are interested in a particular tree you can locate the block alloted to the genus where the species required will be found.

One would expect with a soil pH of 5.4 to find an excellent

display of rhododendrons and such expectations are amply fulfilled. Superb presentation of these plants in beds of varying contours makes this collection one of the most artistic features in the arboretum. There is something here for all seasons beginning with the delicate shaded rose-pink of the early flowering Bodnant-raised *R*. "Seta"; the mid-season filled with a large bush of *R. yakushimanum* now so popular not to need description, followed by the July flowering *R. ungernii* only slightly earlier than the beautiful white *R. auriculatum*. These are mixed with some of the other peat loving subjects including the large leaved *Pieris formosa* in its type form and the compact white flowered *Leiophyllum buxifolium* var. *prostratum*.

The *Eucalyptus* group, not yet fully representative, includes some interesting species such as *E. nitens* whose hardiness is suspect, *E. cordata* the beauty of Tasmania and *E. johnstonii*, also Tasmanian with colourful red bark. Remembering that this is still a very young arboretum devoid of original natural shelter, its showing of tender items such as these, along with *Embothrium, Magnolia, Ginkgo* and others, is a most remarkable achievement.

The Phenological garden here is one of five in the country, and while this is of the greatest interest to plant scientists others too may find some fascination in this study of plant behaviour. Studies are mainly concerned with plant reaction to different climatic conditions. One of the more discernible observations relates to different times of flowering. The results when tabulated are then sent to be monitored at the headquarters of the project in Western Germany.

A general view of the plant collection and surrounding countryside may be obtained from the hill overlooking the arboretum. This is called Slieve Coillte and a motor road reaches almost to the summit. On the way up acre plots of different trees may be observed. These include *Picea omorika, Pinus pinea, Abies alba*, all European species, and near the top *Pinus mugo* which it was hoped was a dwarf form. Unfortunately the growth rate indicates that this is not the case. Problems may therefore arise with these trees restricting if not cutting out the view from this angle. From the highest elevation an excellent view takes in the confluence of the rivers Barrow and Suir before they flow into the sea.

For those coming here to study trees or shrubs the labelling is near perfect. Each group of three carries at least one label and this is placed facing a certain direction so that after finding the first all others will be found in a similar location. Maps are also available which show the placing of the various groupings. The majority who choose this arboretum for an outing will find much pleasure in rambling in pleasant surroundings with the blends of colour skilfully devised to hold their attention. There are also full cafe facilities available near the reception centre.

Johnstown Castle

County Wexford

Johnstown Castle, Co Wexford
Telephone: 053 / 42888

Take the road south from Wexford for about two miles (3 Km)
and follow signposts for Johnstown.

The principal role of Johnstown is that of a research centre, for which purpose it was handed over to the Department of Agriculture in 1948, and was then used primarily as a soil testing station. Ten years later, it was placed under the control of the newly formed Agricultural Institute, an autonomous body having seven main research centres under its control, with a co-ordinating headquarters in Dublin. The Agricultural Institute was subsequently amalgamated with ACOT, forming the new Agriculture and Food Development Authority—Teagasc.

Johnstown is said to be named after King John, who was around these parts in the early 13th century. Earlier it was acquired, by what means is not disclosed, by the Esmonde family and later lost to Cromwell, who installed one of his followers there. It then followed a rather peculiar history since its owners had the uncanny knack of failing to produce heirs, so that although a descendency does exist, this was only maintained by marriage. The final chapters of its family history saw the estate inherited by the late Lady Maurice Fitzgerald from her mother. The last transfer was to a grandson, who gifted the estate to the Irish Government in 1945 to be used for the development of agriculture. The castle itself is not open to the public; its elegant drawingroom, situated on the second floor, commands a view down onto the lake and adjoining lawns similar to that once enjoyed by Powerscourt, which is no coincidence, as both were landscaped by Daniel Robertson.

With the great emphasis on environmental protection, Johnstown Castle has now been given a major national role in investigating this important area of research and conversation. The administrators of this research centre have been quick to recognise the environmental value of the castle's gardens in catering for the needs of those who have become conscious of the confinement of an urban society.

Johnstown can lay no claim to any great gardening tradition. It had what most great houses of its period possessed, a large walled garden distanced from the castle which was flanked by formal lawns. The grounds were laid out to facilitate field sports, lakes well stocked with fish and vast areas of laurel planted to provide ornamental pheasant cover. The removal of large areas of this laurel was one of the first tasks undertaken by the garden staff when the estate passed into public ownership. This has now been achieved and it can be seen retreating into the background, the cleared areas becoming available for new plantings of trees and shrubs.

Inside the castle entrance a planting of lime trees bordering the avenue is widely spaced and set well back, unlike many unfortunate plantings of these trees which crowd out all views and present a dense and rather gloomy coverage. In front of the castle stands an old-style fountain reconstructed by the College of Technology, Bolton Street, Dublin.

Beyond and to the right of the castle an expanse of lawn, termed the Pigeon Meadow for some unrecorded reason, has a backing of some of the oldest plantings around the gardens. *Cupressus macrocarpa* have reached large dimensions, but storm damage has resulted in shattered and twisted limbs. These trees are reputed to be the first planting of the species in Ireland. A large well preserved monkey puzzle, *Araucaria araucana,* is estimated to be around 124 years.

A number of new plantings are promising well, though few of the more tender species have yet been attempted. *Eucryphia glutinosa* was chosen as the subject for a 25th anniversary planting. Other plantings appear to have been carefully chosen. The colourful *Picea likiangensis* should be in all conifer collections and *Picea glauca* var. *albertiana* is an uncommon variety of the white spruce. The very large *Abies procera* "Glauca", a blue version of the better-known noble fir is one of the garden's best specimens.

At the castle end of the lake where formerly there stood a boathouse, a recumbent *Cryptomeria japonica* now lies in the water apparently growing away quite happily, providing an inviting resting site for the resident moorhens and mallard. This artificial five acre lake is not very deep and holds much bird life. The introduction of more mallard to assist in controlling the water weed has not been a complete success.

Opposite the lake the remains of the old ruined Rathlannon Castle, now without a roof but still retaining the stairway which provided access to its four floors, is at least 200 years older than the earliest Johnstown building which was a simple castle tower. The trees in the area west of the ruined castle include three fine fern-leaved beech, *Fagus sylvatica* "Aspleniifolia" having very distinctive cut and lobed rather thin leaves. The sheet of white tiers presented by a large *Viburnum plicatum* forma *tomentosum* probably offers greater popular appeal. An even more graceful effect is presented by the well developed *Cornus kousa*, its boughs weighed down with colourful white bracts tinged with pink.

The clear stemmed Scots pine standing at the left of the driveway is worthy of attention since it has been classed by the Forestry Department as a "mother tree", meaning that seed is being used from this tree to obtain a cultivar improvement of the species.

At the gateway to the walled garden, two fine shrubs should not be missed. Both are southern hemisphere shrubs, both are tender but both are worth attempting in any garden. *Drimys winteri* from South America gives delicately scented white flowers at a moderately early age. The other in complete contrast is Australian and red in flower, *Callistemon citrinus* better known as the bottlebrush.

The four acre walled garden was created in 1844, but its original glass-houses which included a vinery have been taken down and replaced by a modern plant house. The main feature of the garden is a centre walk dividing twin borders backed by clipped yew hedges. These were originally planted with herbaceous material but became so weed-infected that all the plants were removed and the ground cleared. The herbaceous border has now been restored. The two large plots on either side have been grassed down and no doubt will be furnished with shrubs later.

The glasshouse against the south facing wall is fitted with a varied collection of house plants, some of which are on sale from the propagating houses in the yard behind. Decorative hanging baskets suspended from the roof contain the white scented *Jasminum polyanthum*. Against the walls, the equally heavily scented Madagascar jasmine *Stephanotis floribunda* with white trumpet shaped flowers twines itself around supports. Another tropical African shrub *Cassia didymobotrya* provides further wall decoration with racemes of yellow flowers. A young banana plant growing in a terra cotta pot was a present from a neighbouring progressive gardener and is indicative of the standard of Wexford gardens.

Avondale

County Wicklow

Avondale, Rathdrum, Co Wicklow
Telephone: 0404 / 46111

From Dublin take the road south to Wexford for 30 miles (49 Km) to Rathnew. Then turn right for Rathdrum (8.5 miles, 14 Km). The gardens are situated 1 mile (1.5 Km) south of Rathdrum. Alternatively, Rathdrum may be approached from Glendalough. It is 8 miles (13 Km) south.

Avondale, the former residence of Charles Stewart Parnell, was acquired by the British Government in 1904, when a forestry school of small dimensions was established here to provide a nucleus of officers for the infant forestry service. It continued to fulfil this role with interruptions through the years and in 1969 an annex was added to the main house where refresher courses still continue to be held. Apart from its teaching function, Avondale with its 500 acres is perhaps the most important of the country's forestry stations, housing as it does a collection of trees of both historic and economic importance.

The history of Avondale as an arboretum begins with its purchase by a dedicated dendrologist, Samuel Hayes, who built the present house in 1777 and commenced planting on a unprecedented scale. He planted 2,550 beech trees alone, for which he was awarded a medal by the Royal Dublin Society. Incidentally, this was not an unusual gesture by the RDS, who were then under obligation to promote agriculture and free planting and were in receipt of around £5,000 from the Exchequer. A few of these old beeches are still to be seen scattered through the woods. The preserved trunk of one fallen specimen is maintained in a horizontal position alongside the avenue close to the house. The ring count on this tree is 238.

On the death of its first owner in 1795, Avondale passed to Sir John Parnell, a member of an English family from Cheshire who had settled in Queen's County, now Laois. The family continued in residence at Avondale, filling the role of typical country gentry and in 1846 Charles Stewart Parnell was born.

There is no evidence that when Charles Stewart came to inherit the estate he displayed any interest whatever in its timber except as a commercial product, which he exploited by setting up a sawmill, the remains of which may still be seen.

In 1904 the estate, then owned by a Dublin butcher, was sold to the British Government, under whose administration planting recommenced. Many experimental plots were laid down in the next few years by A.C. Forbes, the Director of Forestry in Ireland, who sought and gained the advice of that famous botanist and plant collector Augustine Henry, some of whose own introductions still feature in a secluded grove.

In close proximity to the house and quite apart from the aboretum there are a number of trees and shrubs of considerable interest. Outside the front door a very shapely columnar *Chamaecyparis lawsoniana* "Wisselii" is an inspiring sight when its dark red spring flowers cover the tree. This is a bonus given to growers of this tree here, since on the Continent it never carries this display of male flowers.

Three other great trees exist at Avondale. One, a *Cupressus arizonica*, recorded by Alan Mitchell in 1968 as measuring 77 feet with a girth of 28 inches, ranks as the largest specimen of this species in these islands. The other two are silver firs, *Abies alba,* standing near the edge of the lower pathway. These measure 143 feet, with a girth of almost 6 feet.

The long grass lawn in front of the house is bordered on both sides by many fine shrubs, including the rare *Kalopanax pictus,* comparable to the acers but having large 12 inch leaves and flat white flower heads. The spectacular *Holodiscus discolor* was something I was not expecting to see. Its large panicles of white flowers borne in late July should make this a very popular shrub, but it only appears in four other Irish gardens.

A large bush of *Drimys winteri* has reached about 20 feet, which in view of the shrub failures here is most unexpected. This list records seven planting of *Ginkgo biloba* all of which are now dead. Of seven *Pinus tabuliformis* planted in 1924 none have survived. *Gymnocladus, Eucryphia* and *Sophora* are all recorded as non-survivors. Yet this park cannot be more than fifteen miles from the sea. Perhaps the reason for these failures lies in the low elevation of Avondale which is tucked into a valley producing a frost pocket in which early growths must inevitably be exposed to risks. It is also possible that, during the transition period when Avondale was uncared for, many of these casualties occurred, because when one looks around and sees such items as *Crinodendron*, *Cornus capitata* and *Griselinia* reaching heights of 15 feet it becomes inconsistent to see *Chiosya ternata* and *Garrya elliptica* placed in the list of plants that have not succeeded here.

The large walled garden behind the house now serves as a small deer park. At the rear a short path leads down to Lovers Leap, a vantage point overlooking the river and its timbered valleys below. There is no record of any tragedy ever having occurred here, but any frustrated lover could well imagine this leap led to a sylvan paradise. Through this wooded valley runs a totally concealed railway line which when laid cost the company £3,000 in compensation to the Parnell estate. Unseen trains come rushing through the forest in a most necromantic manner.

The forest plots are set out on either side of a 200 foot-wide Grand Ride ending at a cairn of stones, set up in 1908 from which a wide view of the valley and hills beyond may be obtained. These plots were planned and set up by A.C. Forbes from 1905 onwards.

The Continental Forest Garden design has been used whereby one specimen tree stands in front of the main plot each roughly one acre. Unfortunately nurse trees, often Norway spruce and European larch were used to interplant and protect the more delicate species. Normally this would create no problems but the hiatus which occurred during World War I and after Avondale fell into the ownership of the Irish Government who at that time had no funds to maintain it, resulted in the total neglect at a time when thinning of these nurses should have been undertaken. The damage has never been repairable and in some plots the nurses are dominant.

The influence of Augustine Henry in these plantings is marked by a memorial stone behind which a grove of some of his introductions bears tribute to his work. These include *Pinus armandii* and *Rhododendron henryi*. Another of his discoveries is *Tilia oliveri*, which in 1888 he found in central China. This lime has ovate pale fresh-green leaves, silvery white underneath and glabrous young shoots. The varieties planted in the deciduous section include Spanish chestnut, oak in variety, limes, hornbeam producing very clean slim stems, elm, maples, ash and beech. New plots have been added of *Nothofagus* (southern beech) and walnut.

The conifer section of the forest plots follows the broad leaved trees. All the more commonplace forest trees are included with many additional species not yet in commercial usage. The *Abies* section includes *A. concolor* var. *lowiana* and *A. nordmanniana*. In the *Picea* grouping are many trees more usually associated with arboreta. The elegant *P. smithiana* usually presented in isolation to display its long trailing branchlets can here be seen in massed formation. Likewise *P. omorika* always recognisable by its pagoda like shape and individual character is here growing in compact density similar to that obtaining in its Drina Valley homeland in Yugoslavia.

The most spectacular of the conifer plantings are those on the sloping ground above the river; smooth gun-barrel-like reddish brown trunks of western red cedar, *Thuja plicata*, from a forest floor of *Polystichum* fern. Many of these very fine specimens have been marked out as "mother trees" from which cuttings may be obtained to propagate the cultivar. Rings and numbers denote those trees that have been so selected. Seed is collected between September and February. These magnificant red poles reaching to over 100 feet are only surpassed by their neighbours the sequoias.

The sequoias, more popularly known as redwoods, have been immortalised by the specimens of monumental proportion to be seen in their native California. For a tree capable of living for 3,000 years those growing at Avondale or elsewhere in the British Isles are still in their childhood. Both *Sequoiadendron giganteum* and *Sequoia sempervirens* are represented here by trees of considerable size. Good specimens of *Cryptomeria japonica*, which bear a superficial resemblance to *S.*

sempervirens, are also on view.

After a brief visit to the riverside, at a point where a small natural strand invites delay to watch the bird life which includes kingfishers and dippers, and the clear cool water in which fish abound, the trek continues with a visit to the *Tsuga* section. These have a good claim to be regarded as the most graceful of all the conifers and they may be on the way to making a reputation for themselves as a dual purpose tree suitable for environmental and commercial planting. Here a remarkable feature is the extent of the regeneration taking place with a complete ground covering of vigorous seedling trees, some approaching thinning size.

Lastly there comes the Arboretum and Pinetum in which may be seen some rare and many very attractive trees. The most illustrious of the trees here, *Cupressus arizonica*, does not in fact have a plaque to reveal that this is the tallest of the species in these islands. There is also a particularly fine specimen of *Athrotaxis selaginoides*, the tallest growing of these Tasmanian cedars. The Japanese *Picea koyamae* is also deserving of mention. This is a rare tree both in its native habitat and also in cultivation. Planted in 1910, it had reached a height of 42 feet when last measured in 1976.

This historical arboretum with its colourful history now atracts in excess of 100,000 visitors a year. To those interested in timber trees in all stages of development it provides a fascinating study. Plantsmen and nature lovers will also find here in its exotic specimens much to attract. It can be reached in an hour's drive from Dublin passing through the highly scenic Wicklow countryside.

Killruddery

County Wicklow

Killruddery, Bray, Co Wicklow
Telephone: 01 / 863405

From Dublin take the Wexford road south as far as Bray. The gardens are situated 1.5 miles (2.5 Km) south of Bray on the road to Greystones. They are also served by bus number 84 from Dublin city centre.

Killruddery, on the outskirts of Bray, is one of the very few examples of living history. Not alone can the gardens here lay claim to an existence dating back over 300 years, but this can be matched by the family owning them, who themselves settled here in 1618 and have been in continuous residence ever since. In the world of today where people are moving around like gypsies and even the old landed families are moving out of their estates, the fixity of this family and their surroundings offers a singular appeal.

Until recently, Killruddery was open only to organised parties by prior arrangement, however visitors are now welcomed in the afternoons of three months of the year. Those privileged to visit Killruddery can still move through its seventeenth century surrounds with this original charm in no way debased. This remains a garden still being used by a family who have made similar use of these beautifully landscaped grounds through several centuries. The installation of all the modern paraphernalia which unrestricted public entry would require would destroy much of its nebular charm.

The first house to be built at Killruddery was destroyed during the Civil War of 1645. It was apparently rebuilt by the second Earl of Meath who inherited the house six years later, but the first pictorial recording of this house was not until 1680, when it was shown to be composed of five bays with the frontage facing east. It was at this period, c.1682, that the gardens were laid out at the direction of Monsieur Bonet, a French artist who is said to have received his instruction at Versailles.

The French influence on this garden is still present, along with other European influences, notably Dutch. Statues embellish practically every important landscape feature; many carry the names of the French and German firms that fashioned them.

The gardens are terraced towards their highest point, a large steeply rising bank of rock outcrop providing from its highest elevation a quite magnificent view of the Little Sugar Loaf and Kippure mountains, with woodland and chequered fields sloping back towards the house, which occupies the central position of this far-flung vista. This natural alpine garden invites planting and many plants have been introduced here, including azalea-type rhododendrons, *Juniperus squamata*, *Erica lusitanica*, and *Cotoneaster horizontalis*, but many niches remain which could contain plants.

From this vantage point the lawns stretch almost unbroken back towards the house. To the right near the animal grave mound, a strawberry tree, *Arbutus unedo*, has spread itself over a circumference of 80 yards, with as companion a *Parrotia persica*. Both are subjects for the fading days of autumn, the *Arbutus* both flowering and fruiting and the *Parrotia* displaying its wonderful rich colour range of yellow, pink and crimson. An old world atmosphere is heightened by the pair of mulberries which face each other across the lawn and which were planted in 1908.

On the walk side of this massive lawn a veteran larch, *Larix decidua*, planted in 1750, has a very large quarter girth but a rather blunted top with no leader development. Even this early planting date is still more than 100 years later than the first introduction of this tree from the Carpathians. Nearby a more recent planting of the rarely seen lime *Tilia* "Moltkei", has just reached the stage of maturity when its leaves show their silvery undersides when rustled by the breeze. In this open setting backed by the expanse of lawn, its beauty is further accentuated.

The rock was obviously seized upon by the designer as a focal point with no impediments placed between it and the house, and so it remains to this day. Near the perimeter the outline may still be seen of the old coach road to Bray. Fortunately today the road now runs behind the rock at a distance well removed from the garden.

Two parallel water canals known as the Long Ponds face towards the south side of the house. These measure 550 feet long by 60 feet wide and are similar in design to ones at the Chateau de Courances 50 kilometres south of Paris. It appears that the idea behind this design was to mirror the house in the placid water from which arises the name bestowed upon them: Miroirs d'Eau. It has also been suggested that these were used at some stage to provide a stock of fish for the house, in a manner similar to the fish ponds often associated with monasteries. Today water lilies are well established in one of these ponds while the water in the other remains clear.

Separating the garden from the adjoining fields, is an entrenchment, similar in design to the shallow sunken fence arrangement known as a "ha ha". This was designed to conduct water, and is known as the Stops. It may be presumed that this name arose from the introduction of varying levels which caused the water to be temporarily arrested at various points. A pond known as the Ace of Clubs was incorporated in this waterway. The water serving the Stops, the canals and other pools in the garden comes from a source half a mile distant and conveyed by aqueduct to the garden. There is no longer sufficient water to normally fill both the lawn canals and the Stops. Beyond the Stops a double avenue of lime trees leads to the estate parkland. The trees still provide an impressive sight.

Yew is a predominant planting throughout these gardens; some of the trees have reached a considerable size and the hedges are in a wholesome condition but demanding in the labour of clipping. Nowhere is this task more demanding than in the Angles. These are tall hedges composed of yew, hornbeam, lime and beech shaped in the form of isosceles triangles and enclosing about half a rood of ground with dividing walks. These were the work of M. Bonet who introduced this form of topiary extravaganza from his native France where it was known as *Patte d' Oie*, the foot of a goose.

The age of this garden is again demonstrated by the avenue

of evergreen oaks, *Quercus ilex*. These were planted just short of three hundred years ago and are still in excellent condition, the foliage showing all the glossiness of young trees. This part of the garden is said to have been used by the monks from Thomas Court monastery as their regular walk at the period c.1200.

This distant part of the gardens formerly contained the Bowling Green, perhaps even phlegmatic bowls players were not permitted to disturb the serenity of the formal lawns. Bowl playing ceased in 1930 when the area was planted with birch and poplar. In the 50-odd years of their existence these poplars have produced tall clean stems of commercial quality timber.

Behind the long ponds a wooded area referred to as the Wilderness is divided by symmetrical walks. Some artistic statuary has been placed at focal points, including a Venus by Kahle of Potsdam.

The French influence is again in evidence in the next feature, a circular pond 60 feet in diameter. The central fountain is surrounded by four statues depicting children at play. A double circle of towering beech hedges planted in 1740, with a passage now almost overgrown running through the centre, surrounds the fountain pool. Originally, windows in the inner beech hedge permitted a view of the fountain jets. Again cast iron French statues by Barbezat of Val-D'Osne depicting the four seasons are set at the entrances to this fine example of French garden art.

The Sylvan Theatre, the most simple in design, is perhaps the most captivating of all the French landscape artistry in these gardens. A bay hedge encloses the little theatre whose tiered grass seats ring the turfgrass stage. Records exist of performances in this Elysian setting, but these seem to have been family and private showings rather than public events. A theatre where the sky is the roof maybe carries too many risks for a wary Irish audience. For many a year the only audience has been the four sandstone Muses who view proceedings from the back of the stage.

Closer to the house the two *parterre* 19th century gardens look almost apologetic for intruding upon the more sombre setting of an earlier generation. No longer decked out in the gaudy flower style of the Victorian age, they have reached a compromise with their surrounds by being replanted with small shrubs and herbaceous oddments. The Victorian gardens in their own age were an artistic triumph, but belonged to an era when their upkeep, requiring the expenditure of much labour, was of no consequence. It is a tribute to the owners of this garden that ways have been found to preserve these period gardens and to reclothe them in an ingenious manner with material not in accordance with their intended design, but sufficiently close not to be incongruous.

Those nearest to the house have been accorded more informality and have been planted with a mixture of dwarf shrubs such as fuchsias, species roses, hydrangeas and the lovely sky blue *Ceratostigma* with a mixture of herbaceous plants. The lower garden, its beds backed by scalloped yew hedges and edged with box, has a more formal planting theme confined to a pattern of pale pink roses and lavender. But more importantly, the geometric designs have been carefully preserved in both cases.

In this same area the old ornamental dairy designed by Sir George Hodson gives an excellent impression of a garden teahouse. The solid undressed oak door is cased in cut granite panels. Its cool interior is shaded with stained glass windows under which the slate shelves alone proclaim its purpose was that of a dairy, for which it was used until relatively recently.

On the wall above the dairy a fine specimen of *Magnolia grandiflora*, resplendent with its 10-inch creamy-white flowers, is a plant which alone brings distinction to any garden. Here in the setting of this stately house, it has all the qualities of an architectural plant. A nearby *Myrtus apiculata* flowers and sets fruit in profusion.

The Florence Court yews, *Taxus baccata* "Fastigiata", which line the pathway below the statue gallery have suffered some damage from wind and snow but are now wired to prevent further spreading. New growth will soon cover this temporary blemish and it is more than likely that given this aid, the trees will bond again and present their typical groomed appearance. Curiously enough the more vulnerable incense cedar *Calocedrus decurrens* presents an impeccable columnar green profile. So often this tree is browned by prevailing winds.

At the time of writing, these beautiful grounds are open between 1 and 5 p.m. during May, June and September, and at other times to small groups by prior arrangement.

Kilmacurragh

County Wicklow

Kilmacurragh, Co Wicklow
Telephone: Information from 01 / 867751

From Dublin take the Wexford road south for 30 miles (49 Km)
as far as Rathnew. Turn left at The Tap pub some 5 miles (8
Km) south of Rathnew. Turn left again at the T-junction 1.5
miles (2.5 Km) further on. The entrance to the gardens is on the
left about 500 yards (440 m) from the T-junction. Bus number
84 from Dublin city centre.

This could be the sad account of another once proud Irish garden fallen into desolation. A series of tragedies followed by a lengthy period of neglect have stripped Kilmacurragh of many of its one-time trappings. Yet so much remains to stir memories of what must have ranked as one of the country's foremost gardens; a *Magnolia campbellii* almost the size of a forest oak, a pathway overhung with towering *Rhododendron arboreum*, their falling crimson petals as symbolic as Flanders poppies of a world that has departed. Today Kilmacurragh is owned by the Forest and Wildlife Service who are breathing new life into its old bones. Many old scars remain, but a new purpose has entered this old demesne, and with that purpose an equal determination that what remains of the past will not be permitted to suffer further deterioration.

The Acton family settled at Kilmacurragh around 1690 and continued in direct succession until Thomas Acton, a bachelor, came into possession in the early years of the 19th century. He was succeeded by a nephew who was killed in the first World War in 1915. Tragedy struck again when his brother who inherited the property was himself killed the following year in the battle of Ypres. Family finances were now put under strain, and Kilmacurragh drifted into disrepair until 1920, when it was rented to a German called Budina who ran the place as a hotel and had a ballroom built in the garden area to the rear of the house. This has since been demolished and no traces remain. At the outbreak of the second World War Herr Budina went off to fight for the Fatherland leaving behind him Mr O'Connor as co-trust manager. In 1950 Herr Budina reappeared on the scene, but now a dispute developed over ownership with the two partners at variance. Eventually the place was put on the market and bought by the Government in 1975 who handed 100 acres including the arboretum over to the Department of Fisheries and Forestry to be used as a forestry research station.

A notice on the front door of the mansion, gutted by fire some years previous to the takeover, proclaims that it is under renovation. It is a building of distinction reminiscent in some ways of a Russian style though in fact Queen Anne, low in profile with two wings and a Palladian top frontage. Unfortunately the notice of intent to renovate is more a wish than an intent, no money at present being forthcoming to make restoration possible. The old walled garden is now grassed down to lawns, on which are set the administration buildings of the Forestry Research Unit and also a series of polythene tunnels in which experiments on seedling forest trees are being monitored.

All the old trees in good health have been retained, their identities have been established and they are now furnished with labels. The most remarkable is a truly huge *Magnolia campbellii* growing against the wall with a girth of around 8 feet and a height in excess of 45 feet. A specimen of this tree first flowered in Ireland in 1895, and here we may have another with a comparable date of introduction. There is also an unusual group of three gnarled *Ginkgo*, veterans in appearance but never apparently having achieved an even average growth rate. In the arboretum outside, many old relics remain including the tender *Cupressus cashmeriana*, one of the most decorative of the conifers. Another shrub indicative of the quality of this collection is the pink spring-flowering *Dipelta ventricosa*. This deciduous Chinese shrub is quite hardy, but although introduced in 1904, does not often appear in cultivation. *D. yunnanensis* is present in the Glasnevin and Mount Usher collections. Nothing gives greater character to this garden than the double row of *Rhododendron arboreum* running the length of the central pathway, which following their flowering is carpeted with pink petals.

Several of the trees have received mention by writers on

conifers. The late Tony Hanan, himself a member of the Forestry Service, notes a record *Athrotaxis laxifolia* and a good *A. cupressoides*. He also mentions a *Fitzroya cupressoides* now 58 feet. Alan Mitchell in his record of arboreta credits Kilmacurragh with 39 outstanding conifers, of which a fair number still survive including *Saxegothaea conspicua, Podocarpus salignus, Cryptomeria japonica* with its variety "Elegans" forming a vast clump in front of the house. But undoubtedly the most interesting of all the trees here is that clone discovered by the Acton family and named *Chamaecyparis lawsoniana* "Kilmacurragh", marked by its narrow columnar habit and variation of foliage colour. A specimen growing close to the road is said to be the original.

Since my first visit to Kilmacurragh in 1984 much clearance of scrub has taken place, revealing many more unusual trees and shrubs dating back to the Acton plantings from 1850 onwards to his death in 1908.

Within the walled garden close to the gigantic *Magnolia campbellii*, a *Lardizabala biternata* has emerged making a very rewarding display of its chocolate-purple flowers during the winter months. This plant is only recorded in three other Irish gardens. A 20 foot *Embothrium coccineum* is recorded as having been planted in 1876, which now provides a spectacular display with its scarlet flowers in late May. The rarest and very tender southern beech *Nothofagus moorei,* from New South Wales has now attained 30 feet.

Some exciting conifers have also been rescued from the engulfing jungle. These include the very elegant *Cupressus cashmeriana*, unfortunately delicate but undoubtedly the most beautiful conifer in existence. The 30-foot tree here is perhaps around 100 years of age. *Fitzroya cupressoides* also claims attention; at 58 feet this is the tallest living recording of this tree in Ireland. It is more often seen as a shrub rather than a tree. A mention must also be accorded to *Picea polita* often alluded to as the tiger tailed spruce because of its densely clothed pendulous branchlets, for some an irresistible attraction. Other notable plants more in evidence are the cork oak *Quercus suber* of economic interest, and the most extraordinary tree of all,

Pseudopanax crassifolius, ignored by anyone seeking beautiful plants but adored by many people because of its grotesque appearance. Its long, heavily serrated sword-like leaves stand out stiffly, falling away as the tree grows until it finishes as a tall clean stalk with a mop head top. Liberties should not be taken with the 18-foot *Umbellularia* whose heavy load of green foliage will if bruised and inhaled produce headaches and faintness.

The public interest in Kilmacurragh is probably twofold. There are those who would be primarily interested in its history as a great Irish garden and would welcome the opportunity to see what remains of its collection of trees and shrubs. These were still of sufficient interest to attract a visit from the International Dendrology Society on their recent Irish tour. There are others including amateurs and professionals who would wish to inspect the scientific work being carried on here.

But it must be stressed that this is a research station and as such must observe certain safeguards. Public entry to Kilmacurragh is restricted but the director in charge states that those who have an interest scientific or otherwise in seeing around the place would be welcome. Those wishing to avail of this kindness should seek permission in advance, preferably attaching themselves to groups who can be shown around in the same time that would be taken up with one individual.

Mount Usher

County Wicklow

Mount Usher Gardens, Ashford, Co Wicklow
Telephone: 0404 / 40116

The gardens are in the village of Ashford 28 miles (45 Km) south of Dublin on the main road to Wexford. They can be reached by bus number 84 from Dublin city centre.

Beautiful Mount Usher benefits from a combination of naturally occurring amenities, water, shelter and unusually local climatic conditions. These, in addition to a great deal of care, have helped to make Mount Usher one of the most popular of the gardens of Ireland. The foundations laid by the first of the Walpole family, who in 1860 purchased the old mill and one acre which he proceeded to plant, were to be built upon by the three generations of garden lovers who followed. This continuity of effort has raised Mount Usher to its present pinnacle of garden perfection.

In 1981 the gardens, comprising 20 acres passed out of the hands of the Walpole family and were acquired by their present owner, Mrs Jay. It might be assumed that anyone seeking to possess a garden of national importance such as Mount Usher would have a long dedicated association with the pursuit of gardening. Mrs Jay, however, admits to no such attachment. In fact she denies any apprenticeship to the art of gardening. So it is all the more laudable that she should have come to the rescue of Mount Usher when no other buyers were in sight and an indifferent Irish Government was prepared to let this national heritage fall prey to development speculators.

Approached from Dublin, the garden entrance is on the Wicklow side of the village of Ashford. The quadrangular area inside the entrance gate bordered by high beech hedges is the main herbaceous area of the garden. In addition a collection of dwarf conifers contains many of distinction. Mistletoe has colonised some of the old apple trees in the left hand corner.

Turning right through the beech archway at the far end of

this enclosure leads to the Banana Belt where banana plants of an Indian variety are growing luxuriantly but as yet have produced neither flowers nor fruit. Further along, sheltered by brick wall abutments, are several interesting plants including *Feijoa sellowiana* from Brazil, now renamed *Acca sellowiana*, and *Pseudopanax crassifolius*. This is an unusual New Zealand tree with a ten foot bare stem surmounted by a cluster of sword-like leaves, fifteen inches or more in length and deeply serrated. Around the corner a well developed *Magnolia campbellii* flowers every alternate year.

Back to the lawn below the suspension bridge the Australian *Leptospermum* cover themselves in vivid carmine blooms during May and June. In the woodland above, an assortment of rhododendrons show their varying range of colours. In the corner of the glade below the woodland, beside the old croquet ground, may be seen *Cunninghamia lanceolata* planted in 1875, now 75 feet in height. This Chinese conifer is, perhaps, apart from the *Eucalyptus* and *Pinus montezumae* the finest plant in the Mount Usher collection.

Close by there is a large specimen of *Umbellularia californica* flowering in April, but more noteworthy because of the overpowering effect of the aroma from the crushed leaves. On the opposite side stands the original *Pinus montezumae*, 66 feet tall and planted in 1909, and from the seed of which a second generation was raised in 1927-8. This Mexican Pine with its eight inch long blue needle leaves will arrest your attention.

A little apart will be seen a *Podocarpus salignus*, an attractive member of this genus of conifers from Chile giving an almost tropical effect with its pendulous dark green foliage. On the opposite side of the glade are a solid bank of *Eucryphia glutinosa*. Across the river may be seen *E.* X *nymansensis* "Mount Usher". This is of the same parentage as *E.* X *nymansensis* "Nymansay", but it would appear that the Mount Usher variety was again crossed back to *E. cordifolia*, one of its original parents. These may be seen in flower in late summer or early autumn. *E. moorei* was still in bloom in late October.

At the end of the glade on re-entering the woodland the great eucalypts of Mount Usher tower over 100 feet above. Two trees of *E. viminalis* particularly stand out with ghostly white trunks reaching 118 feet into the sky. This is one of the eucalypts that the koalas feed upon. In the same category is *E. urnigera* at 135 feet. Both of these are Tasmanian species, and here without question is the finest collection of these southern hemisphere trees to be found in Ireland.

Before leaving this area time should be spared for a glimpse of the *Wisteria sinensis* which has attained the summit of a large Lawson cypress, from which it hangs in great cascades. This will be found near the boundary fence.

Next a pause should be made while crossing the river bridge to view a very fine *Metasequoia glyptostroboides* on the right bank looking towards the house. This conifer was known only in its fossilised form until the discovery of a living specimen in central China in 1941. Here is a really good specimen obviously relishing its siting close to the river. On dry sites these trees can disappoint and may even fail to survive.

Over the river a good example of *Chamaecyparis lawsoniana* "Kilmacurragh" may be seen on the right. This tall graceful spire has gained popularity through its proven hardiness and resistance to snow. Here also is a shrub looking like a holly but which is *Desfontainia spinosa*, a South American shrub which covers itself with long tubular yellow-orange flowers. It is not quite hardy but will succeed in most locations. Nearby can be seen a southern hemisphere conifer of outstandingly beautiful form, *Austrocedrus chilensis*. Further along on the right another rare conifer presents itself, *Picea morrisonicola* from Taiwan. Opposite is one of the South American beeches, *Nothofagus dombeyi*, one of twelve members of this genus to be found in this garden.

Another strange shrub met with here is *Colletia cruciata* from Uruguay, an unendearing looking shrub armed with sharp spine-like leaves which carry white pitcher shaped flowers, scented with coconut. Perhaps more attractive is the golden chestnut, *Chrysolepis chrysophylla*, a member of the Fagaceae, with leaves dark green on top and yellow underneath and fruits produced in prickly clusters.

On the lawn below the house may be seen an outstanding plant of *Cornus alternifolia* "Argentea", its branches spread in flat layers carrying the beautiful silver-variegated leaves. It resembles *C. controversa* "Variegata" but is more dainty in habit. Above this, beneath the house, is *Myrtus apiculata,* a Chilean myrtle flowering in summer and autumn. In this same area is a very remarkable shrub called *Emmenopterys henryi,* a rare Chinese tree which has only once, since its introduction in 1907, been seen to flower in any part of the British Isles. This was at Wakehurst gardens in Sussex. Another rarity seen here is *Franklinia alatamaha,* formerly known as *Gordonia alatamaha,* bearing white *Stuartia*-like flowers. It was native to North America, but now only exists in cultivation.

On the driveway after passing the house may be seen the redwood tree *Sequoia sempervirens,* planted in 1860 and now 75 feet tall. Proceeding down the right hand river bank *Magnolia* X *veitchii* claims attention in spring with its thousands of purple-pink flowers borne on naked stems. Further along on the opposite bank can be seen *Acer grosseri* var. *hersii,* one of the marbled bark maples with rich autumn colour.

On the fence side of the walk on the opposite bank a good specimen of *Decaisnea fargesii,* a Chinese shrub, claims attention by its attractive seed pods of metallic blue the size of broad beans. Again approaching the suspension bridge, the less-common of the swamp cypresses, *Taxodium ascendens,* may be seen close by the river. The tassel-like branches are vivid green when young, but colour to a rich russet in late autumn. Even more spectacular colouring is provided by the rich scarlet autumn tints of *Nyssa sylvatica,* commonly known as the tupelo tree.

The trees given a mention are but a tiny fraction of those contained in this massive collection, probably unparalleled in any other Irish garden. For those well versed in botany this garden is one of absorbing interest. For others it provides unsurpassed beauty and colour in the variety of its plants with the added attraction of the river Vartry, which runs through the length of the garden, falling over a succession of built up weirs. Pollution, one hopes, will never come to ruin this panoramic scene as it has done to so many other Irish waterways. The labelling in this garden is excellent and no visitor will have any difficulty identifying the plants.

Powerscourt

County Wicklow

Powerscourt Demesne, Co Wicklow
Telephone: 01 / 867676

Drive south from Dublin 13 miles (21 Km) to Enniskerry. The well signposted gardens are one mile (1.5 Km) south of the village of Enniskerrry. Powerscourt is served by bus number 44 from Dublin city centre.

Twelve miles from Dublin, set in a recess off the main Wicklow road on the outskirts of Enniskerry, Powerscourt occupies a unique niche in the top division of Irish gardens. Reminiscent of some of the great country houses of England, where landscaping holds priority over the more usual style of informal gardening, Powerscourt does not fit easily into the concept of an Irish garden. Here everything else is subordinated to the three dimensional artistry aimed to create the sublime setting for a stately home.

Using the backdrop of the Sugar Loaf mountain, the viewer is led over elaborate terraces studded with the ornamentation of statuary, crafted ironwork and water. Lateral depth is obtained by the vast amphitheatre with all trees thrust back into the role of an unobtrusive framing. Daniel Robertson was one of many designers who contributed to the magnificence of Powerscourt.

A century earlier that asymmetrical advocate Richard Payne Knight would have regarded Powerscourt with some distaste. Dendrologists will probably find the framing more interesting than the picture, while thousands of other viewers will acclaim this epic of landscaping.

The entrance to the estate is through a winding avenue of clean-stemmed beeches mostly planted over 200 years ago and now in decline. Passing the shell of the burnt out mansion, its tiny cannon defiantly in position, a left turn reveals the forecourt of the garden centre where a very comprehensive selection of plants is on offer for sale.

To the right of the sales area an impressive but sombre

avenue of *Araucaria araucana* leads to a pedestal-mounted statue of Ajax, the handsome warrior. The planting of this avenue could date back to about 1870. At present prices of £12 a tree this would be a costly exercise.

On the opposite side of this avenue a lavishly ornate gate taken from a cathedral in Bavaria leads into a large lawn area dominated by two statues in bronze of the Herculaneum "Ball Throwers". A gateway in the centre leads to what was formerly the kitchen garden, but which now possesses only a central walk flanked by two newly designed herbaceous borders; the remaining space being given over to commercial horticulture, with fruit trees growing on the red brick walls.

At the end of this walk a feature gateway, with emblems representing Ireland, England, Scotland and Wales, leads into an American-type garden planted with some interesting trees and shrubs. On the wall close to the gateway the lovely *Myrtus apiculata* with its peeling cinnamon coloured inner surface, shows white scented flowers in late summer and autumn. The trees here include the giant fir of North America, *Abies grandis,* with bright green leaves, and *Chamaecyparis nootkatensis,* one of the parents of that infant prodigy of the conifer world X *Cupressocyparis leylandii,* so useful for providing quick shelter.

Unhappily placed in these shady surroundings is that rarity of Irish gardens the black mulberry *Morus nigra,* seen at its best in the Botanical Gardens, Glasnevin. A large specimen of the tree rhododendron *R. arboreum* overlooks the lake. The colour of the large tight trusses may vary from near white to deep blood red, and equally variable is the time of flowering which may extend from January to April.

Further down the slope a very large *Drimys winteri* is encountered which, it is claimed, Alan Mitchell has described as the best in Europe. Perhaps he is right, but other large specimens of this species do exist, including one over fifty feet high at Kilmacurragh. Size may depend upon variety as botanists are now inclined to divide this species into three varieties, based largely on geographical distribution. Strangely enough the larger growing trees are those from the most southerly and colder latitudes below 40° South. The white one and a half inch diameter flowers are quite fragrant and a tree generously adorned with these is indeed a glorious sight. The aromatic bark of this tree was used as a remedy for scurvy by sailors under Sir Francis Drake.

Passing by the lake where a copy of a piece of Italian statuary throws a jet of water to nearly one hundred feet, a good view is obtained of the imposing facade of the house surmounting the lofty terraces. Then a descent is made into a lowland area, formerly a piece of bogland, re-structured in 1908 into a semblance of a Japanese garden, where the planting is rather banal, with only a small proportion of the subjects having a Japanese connection.

Amongst the many *Trachycarpus fortunei* palms are scattered some *Viburnum*, *Camellia*, *Prunus* and *Magnolia*, most of them the better known varieties with few rarities. A good *Acer griseum*, the Chinese maple, stands out on the far slope and that graceful Chinese conifer, *Juniperus squamata* "Meyeri" catches the eye. The bamboos here are the large-leaved *Sasa palmata*, quite oblivious to frost.

Climbing out of this pleasant little dell we find ourselves again at the lake side where at the path's edge the native Killarney strawberry tree, *Arbutus unedo*, produces its white flowers and strawberry-like fruits together in the autumn. Close by and obviously enjoying the peaty soil is a good specimen of the Japanese fir *Abies firma*, a confirmed lime hater. The leaves are glossy green with well marked silvery bands of stomata on the under surface. All around this garden there are clumps of *Phormium tenax* of different varieties. These were raised from seed sent to Powerscourt by that notable connoisseur of rhododendrons, the Earl of Stair.

Leaving the lake side and descending to the valley walk we enter an area populated in some density by a mixture of conifers, some of outstanding size which as individual specimens would present a magnificent sight, but rather overcrowded as a result of their subordinate role in the landscaping scheme. One of these is *Pseudotsuga japonica*, sometimes known as the Japanese douglas fir, which has reached the remarkable height of 60 feet, a record in these islands for this tree of limited stature. The very ornamental *Picea likiangensis* is also here, decked with its brilliant red young cones in May. *Abies nordmanniana* planted in 1867 is now a giant of 90 feet.

Perhaps the most unusual of the conifers here is *Pinus torreyana* coming from the San Diego coast where it is often seen as a small bush, but represented here as a small tree with tufted branchees of five leaves and four inch cones with edible seeds. Another of the pines on view is *P. coulteri*, sometimes referred to as the large-coned pine because of its 10 inch long cones which may weigh as much as five pounds. It is three-leaved with bluish grey colouring. Dr Nelson of Glasnevin Botanical Gardens, writing in *The Garden*, has claimed this tree as the tallest of its species in these islands. Confusion on this point may arise from the R.H.S. publication *Conifers in the British Isles* which lists the Powerscourt tree as 56 feet and the tallest a tree of 100 feet growing at Titley Court in Hereford-shire. The latter tree is however now dead and, as Dr Nelson claims, the title has passed on to the Powerscourt tree. But this tree has proved to be of very short life span; of the thirteen large trees measured in 1909 none now survive, so this Powerscourt tree may be approaching its final years.

On the way up the slope to the Pepper Pot tower the beautiful golden larch, *Pseudolarix amabilis*, a rather difficult tree to establish, finds conditions here to its liking but it is never a big grower. From the tower itself a good view is obtained of the big deep-blue Cedar, *Cedrus atlantica* forma *glauca;* and beside the containing walls the round symmetry of the tower is mirrored by the sentinel Italian *Cupressus sempervirens* which surround it. Form over the adjoining wall hangs another *Arbutus* not worried by its windswept position.

Back to the house the full panoramic effect of the grand view presents itself. The viewer will be entranced as the gaze wanders over the cobble stoned patio, across the two bronze winged horses, over the lake and fountain until culminating at the shapely outline of the Sugar Loaf mountain, acting as the focal point of this wide flung vista.

The granite built mansion, whose windows once commanded this exquisite view, was destroyed by fire in 1974 and already seedling trees and the ubiquitous buddleias grow from the crumbling interior walls. The adjoining wing is further embellished by the inspired planting along its entire frontage of a cordon row of *Fremontodendron californicum*. These plants although tender and short-lived are worth growing for their rich butter-yellow floral display from May to July; having no petals the calyx provides the colour.

Before leaving by the Chorus gateway, elegant as the rest, two commemorative trees are noticeable on either side; a *Sequoia sempervirens* planted by Princess Mary in 1911 and on the same occasion a *Cryptomeria japonica* planted by the Prince of Wales, perhaps better known as the Duke of Windsor.

Northern Ireland

Castlewellan

County Down

Castlewellan, Co Down
Telephone: (08) 03967 / 78664

From Newry take the road north east for 19 miles (31 Km) to Castlewellan and follow signposts from there.

Castlewellan, situated in the heart of rural Co Down and formerly owned by the Annesley family, was purchased by the Ministry of Agriculture (Forestry Division) from Mr Gerald Annesley in 1967. The family, which originally sprang from the Lordship of Annesley in Nottingham, had resided here for over 200 years during which time they simultaneously developed the estate and the town. Both reveal the influence of the French architect commissioned to work here.

The castle was built in 1856 by the 4th Earl of Annesley and records reveal that planting commenced c. 1870 and has since proceeded uninterrupted to the present day. The very large walled garden comprising 12 acres dated from 1740 when presumably it was then devoted to the growing of vegetables and choice fruits, with perhaps a portion set aside for producing fresh flowers for the house predating the castle. Today this garden has ceased to serve the needs of a family and has become an enclosure in which are set out a collection of herbaceous plants and shrubs of botanical interest. It is now named the Annesley garden in tribute to the work of the previous owner Mr Gerald Annesley.

The walled garden contains extensive twin herbaceous borders. These, under the terms of the takeover agreement, must be maintained as such in perpetuity resulting in a continuous display of herbaceous material throughout the summer months. A picturesque summer tea house adorns the right hand corner of the garden. This is said to have been designed by Sir Edwin Lutyens.

A touch of originality is seen in the two hedges running

down the centre of the garden, fashioned from *Drimys lanceolata* which provide a wonderful display of copper tinted young growth in late spring. Even with clipping, some flowers will appear providing an extra bonus, but it should not be overlooked that this is an Australian plant which will not stand climates other than those of favoured gardens.

Castlewellan should perhaps be more properly described as an arboretum so great is the preponderance of conifers, some of which have been given prominent positions in this enclosed garden. All are trees of special interest. The Castlewellan form of *Juniperus recurva* growing here is distinguished by its more slender branchlets and softer foliage. Also present is that more tender relation of the Chinese fir, *Cunninghamia konishii*, smaller in habit and in leaf than *C. lanceolata*.

Another of the smaller conifers to be seen here, *Cephala-taxus harringtonia* var. *harringtonia*, has larger leaves than var. *drupacea* and large olive green fruits. In appearance these trees are not unlike *Torreya* and are equally hardy. Then there is an unusual type of our one-time native pine, the Scots pine, here represented in its golden form *Pinus sylvestris* "Aurea". A small young specimen of the big cone pine, *Pinus coulteri* has a place on the lawn. This Californian conifer with its huge cones is very fast growing but has only a limited life span.

The hybrid *Corokia* grown here is perhaps the most florif-erous of this New Zealand genus, producing masses of yellow flowers and later covers itself in bright orange fruits. *C. X virgata* is of erect habit unlike its contorted parent *C. cotoneas-ter*, sometimes dubbed the wire netting bush. A Douglas fir might seem out of place in a walled garden, but the variety here is *Pseudotsuga menziesii* var. *glauca*, the blue form which is much slower growing and indeed sometimes treated as a separate species. The best blue forms make very attractive garden plants.

Outside the walled garden the arboretum covers over 100 acres and contains in addition to its splendid trees a very comprehensive collection of shrubs. In addition to this an extension is envisaged to house a collection of oaks from the U.S.A., and other selected conifers and hardwoods. Areas have been designated to represent the four seasons, providing for a spring garden, adjacent to the Annesley garden, an autumn wood beside the Castle, a winter garden north of the Annesley garden and, of course, the Annesley garden itself with its herbaceous display acting as the summer garden. Besides all these there is also the Cypress Pond containing the *Chamaecyparis* collection.

The importance of the arboretum is perhaps best manifested by the number of trees it contains of outstanding size or rarity. Nowhere else in these islands is there to be found a larger specimen of *Picea spinulosa*, that elegant pendulous spruce comparable to *Picea smithiana*, or of *Pinus sylvestris* "Aurea", already encountered in the Annesley Garden. The *Juniperus recurva*, though not the Castlewellan form, is in the same bracket, and that other beautiful weeper, *Cupressus cashmeriana*, falls only slightly below the record for this species.

Abies fraseri gets a mention in the honours list, with *Abies delavayi* var. *faxoniana* not far behind. It does not of course follow that size is equated to beauty and indeed some of the loveliest items in this collection are of very modest dimensions. Almost all of this garden is completely informal with the neatly clipped grass providing a natural setting for these trees and shrubs, besides affording a pleasant passage for strolling among them.

Eucryphia have been met with in some numbers in most gardens but nowhere else are they seen in such massed effect as in the *Eucryphia* walk in this garden. Most were raised from seed. Among the more interesting varieties represented are a clone of *E. X nymansensis* called "Grahamii" and the very tall *E. cordifolia* a tender evergreen bearing large white flowers. These are found growing in their native habitat of southern Chile mixed with *Nothofagus dombeyi*, also to be found in this collection. Another *Northofagus* growing well here is *N. procera* which can provide significant autumn colour, and unlike *dombeyi* is perfectly hardy.

Of the many conifers here none is more spectacular than *Picea likiangensis* which, loaded in late spring with its brilliant red young cones, is magnificent. But to set out to grow this tree requires patience as coning does not occur on young treees. Less dramatically beautiful but worthy of inclusion in any selective collection, *Pinus patula* has the graceful distinction of all Mexican pines; the thinness of its foliage reveals to better effect the long glaucous green pendulous branchlets.

All conifers have their own special attractions. Here is *Abies delavayi* var. *georgei,* which if one turns back its branchlets will reveal the silvered strips of stomata on the undersurface of the leaves. In this collection of unusual plants it is no surprise to discover *Cornus walteri,* a rather little known member of the cornels, of tree size from west China with white flowers.

To find plants dated always adds to their interest and here a planting date of 1880 for an *Arbutus menziesii* suggests its present height of around 30 feet is nearing its limit. This Californian species of strawberry tree is borderline hardy. Its fruit is more orange than red. Another tender tree in most areas, *Podocarpus dacrydioides,* seems to consider this Co Down climate a fair substitute for its native New Zealand and rewards us with a display of graceful beauty in its pendulous branches of bronze green leaves.

The emphasis laid on the conifers of this arboretum may tend to provide an imbalance in the description of a collection which in fact is very varied indeed. In justification it can be stated that with the decline of Headfort, and with no other comparable rival in sight, Castlewellan is aspirant to the role of the leading conifer collection in Ireland.

It is however fully large enough to contain a wealth of other trees and shrubs. One of these is *Eucalyptus urnigera* whose last recorded measurement stood at 102 feet. This is known as the urn gum in its Tasmanian homeland because of the urn shape of the calyx tube. What better setting than among the conifers could be given to the *Telopea truncata,* carrying its nectar-laden rich crimson flowers in mid summer. This Australian shrub can be classed as hardy given a sheltered position in full sun. Here it is seen as a magnificent specimen of 18 feet, a memorable sight in full flower.

A good collection of rhododendrons have been assembled

here in the spring garden and in the rhododendron wood. One striking representative of the genus is the hybrid *R.* "Crest", a primrose yellow which can trace its ancestry back to *R. wardii*. One more conifer which claims a mention is a remarkable multi-stemmed *Sequoiadendron giganteum*, 67 feet high. The suckering which has produced this cluster of stems is most unusual, although this tree will form roots wherever a low bough makes ground contact.

The arboretum is currently managed by a committee comprised of five members. Four of these, including the resident head forester, Mr Sam Harrison, are appointees of the Ministry of Agriculture, while the fifth is Mr Gerald Annesley, the previous owner whose presence reflects the Ministry's interest in preserving the family connection. Mr Annesley lives four miles away and visits the garden every week.

In addition to the arboretum there is a forest park of over 1,000 acres which probably attracts quite a proportion of the 80,000 visitors who arrive here every year.

Mount Stewart

County Down

Mount Stewart Gardens, Greyabbey, Co Down
Telephone: (08) 024774 / 387

From Belfast take the road east for 9.5 miles (15 Km) to
Newtownards and south from there for 3 miles (5 Km).

This garden is situated on the east shore line of Strangford Lough, five miles south east of Newtownards. The climate here is favourably disposed to the growth of tender plants.

The garden's origins are modern. In 1921 Lady Londonderry had a dream of a garden of magnificent proportions carved out of the damp and dismal surroundings in which she had come to live at Mount Stewart. All of us have dreams, but few are permitted to see their fantasies materialise in the manner that saw the creation of this 75 acre garden, which now ranks among the foremost in the British Isles. Indeed if the garden architecture, the brainchild of this remarkable woman, is considered, Mount Stewart is perhaps the greatest of them all.

The greatest of gardens can quickly fall into decline if continuous care and attention is not forthcoming. It is therefore gratifying to find that under National Trust management this has not happened. Since 1970 the present head gardener, Mr Nigel Marshall has zealously sought to refurnish and redesign those areas of the garden showing decline. In consultation with Mr G.S. Thomas of the National Trust, this dedicated plantsman has insured that this garden will approach the next century unimpaired.

The house, also a Trust property, has been given extensive exterior repairs and is also open to the public. A happy circumstance is that a member of the family, Viscountess Bury, the youngest daughter of the late Edith Marchioness of Londonderry D.B.E., still resides in a portion of the house. This family continuity is always a pleasing feature which softens the transformation of a family home into a museum.

It is perhaps fitting to look first at the Sunk Garden on the west side of the house, since this is known to have been the first area to which Lady Londonderry turned her attention, assisted in its design by Gertrude Jekyll. It was at that time referred to as the Blue Garden, a reference to its colour scheme. Over the years many of the original plants have taken their departure. A new design now features herbaceous plants in mixtures of blue, purple, yellow and orange in the four main beds. Large specimens of the Portuguese heath *Erica lusitanica* ring the area below the steps. The heavy scent of their white flowers pervades this whole area in early spring.

On the top terrace a collection of old roses features those raised by Dicksons and named in this nursery after members of the Londonderry family. Still to be seen is *Rosa* "Lord Castlereagh" a velvet red, *R*. "Lady Helen" another red, and *R*. "The Marchioness of Londonderry" a pure white. Of the more unusual introductions to be seen here are a young plant of the Tasmanian *Acacia riceana* sited towards the end of the raised pavement running along the right hand boundary. This plant has tiny needle-like leaves, and yellow flowers carried freely. Two climbers also deserve attention; *Billardiera longifolia* has summer flowers of little attraction, but covers itself in small shining purple fruits during autumn. The unruly *Lardizabala biternata* is a vigorous climber requiring pruning to maintain control. The flowers concealed under the glossy foliage are delicately proportioned and chocolate purple in colour. This is another plant of late season attraction.

Visitors to the garden will probably first enter the Mairi Garden. This area approached from the Fountain Walk was originally used as a quiet retreat where, as an infant, Lady Mairi, the youngest daughter of Lady Londonderry, was placed in her perambulator to sleep. This inspired her mother to create a small and simple childlike garden in which the colour decor was confined to tones of blue and white. An early addition was the centre lead statue of Lady Mairi with a pool surround. The design of the fountain represents "Mairi, Mairi, quite contrary" of the well-known nursery rhyme. The same theme is extended to the planting, where the "silver bells" are represented by various blue and white campanulas.

Here can be seen the white flowering *Dicentra eximia* var. *alba*, the white rose "Bourbon Boule de Neige" and the sweetly scented, white, June-flowering *Clematis fargesii* var. *souliei*. The large *Eucalyptus globulus* pre-dates the garden with a recorded planting date of 1896. Two other items claiming attention are the well developed *Pittosporum eugenioides* with pale-yellow honey-scented flowers and the New Zealand *Fuchsia excorticata*, distinguished by its alternate leaves.

Emerging onto the Dodo Terrace built in 1925 one is confronted by a series of stone carved animals, a whimsical portrayal of members of a London wartime committee known as the Ark Club, whose members bore the names of real or imaginary animals and met under the patronage of Lady Londonderry. The plants here comprise groups of the very decorative and hardy *Fuchsia* "Mrs Popple and *F.* "Enfant Protigue", and a plant of that very showy tubular red flowered climber *Lapageria rosea* fronted by a spreading *Rhododendron yunnanense*. Further along is a large clump of the South African *Melianthus major*, a sub-shrub with soft pinnate leaves, tropical in effect and with tubular crimson flowers.

Below stretches the more formal Italian Garden extending across the south frontage of the house. The designer's art is again apparent in the artistic blending of house and garden, each complementary to the other. On the wall of the house four tailored *Magnolia grandiflora* "Goliath" provide a touch of floral grandeur. These have been carefully pruned to ensure they do not obscure the windows. An especially good form of *Clianthus puniceus* obtained from a local garden has flowers of a softer pink than the type. Close by a *Rosa gigantea*, removed while the walls were being renovated, is again displaying its climbing vigour. The round-headed *Paulownia tomentosa* provides evidence of an injudicous piece of planting but is now much too large to move to a more suitable site.

The main lawn area of this garden is divided into two separate *parterres* replanted with herbaceous material in keeping with the original design of Lady Londonderry. The two large bay laurels in cut stone tubs were imported from Belgium in 1923 at a cost of £100. Other shrubs of interest in this area are the Chinese *Camellia reticulata* with large dark pink blooms, and a large *Sophora tetraptera* with rich yellow flowers in May. *Camellia sasanqua* is usually given wall protection, but here shows itself happy with overhead cover. Its delicate pinkish white flowers peep shyly from the foliage throughout the winter. Another perpetual flowering performer and also tender grows close by. This is the powder blue *Ceanothus arboreus* "Trewithen Blue", unequalled in colour intensity by any other member of the genus.

Entry to the Lily Wood reveals a very different setting. Here plants mingle in complete informality. A massive *Abies nordmanniana* some 80 feet in height dominates the scene. At ground level many ferns flourish in the cool damp atmosphere. The largest, a *Dicksonia antarctica*, was planted in 1936. A large group of the South American *Blechnum capense* are growing as freely as would the native Irish species *B. spicant*.

The mixture here is fascinating. The rare and tender enjoy the protection afforded by the robust and more ordinary, if indeed there are any of the latter. Perhaps one such is the common laurel, yet how many have seen a laurel with leaves all green on one side of the branch and butter yellow on the other? This freak was found as a single branch growing on a normal laurel and was propagated by Mr Marshall. Such abnormalities are hard to explain, perhaps being of virus origin or maybe a chimera.

A provider of more orthodox beauty is the ten foot *Juniperus recurva,* or the more formal *Cupressus duclouxiana* carrying its tiny round cones at an early age. On the fringes of the wood an *Actinidia chinensis* clambering over a host tree is laden with the brown felted kiwi fruits. Nearby a large *Grevillea sulphurea* gives a rewarding display in mid summer with its canary yellow flowers. A contrast in colour is provided by the Mexican *Abelia* X *grandiflora* with tubular cherry-red flowers. Later flowering, the Chilean hazel *Gevuina avellana* produces white flowers in August, but is equally decorative out of flower with its serrated pinnate leaves up to sixteen inches long.

This area, like most others in the garden, is not without its rhododendrons. A shapely young *R. falconeri* already carrying flowers of creamy yellow with a purple blotch is distinguished by its handsome brown tomentum. Here also may be seen *R. crassum,* regarded as one of the hardier members of the Maddenii series. The flowers are heavily scented, and white with a pinkish tinge.

The neighbouring Shamrock Garden features the famous red hand. The hand set in paving stones is planted with *Begonia semperflorens* in the summer and double red daisies in the spring. Behind, a skilfully executed Irish Harp has been fashioned in yew topiary. Mythological topiary animals flank the sides. A *Mahonia* background of *M. lomariifolia* and its hybrid *M.* "Charity" make an interesting comparison. For spring attraction there are *Hamamelis japonica* var. *arborea, Prunus laurocerasus,* and the camellias *C.* X *williamsii* "J.C. Williams" and *C.* X *williamsii* "St Ewe".

Towards the main drive end of Lily Wood lies the Coronation Glade, an area planted by Lord Londonderry in 1952 to mark the coronation of Queen Elizabeth II. On emerging on to the Drive itself first impressions may be those of disappointments. This was the old main drive to a great house. Such approaches raise expectations of broad landscaping and fine timber. Neither are in evidence, yet there do exist impressive latter day plantings of tree rhododendrons and conifers. All of this does of course fit the picture of the environments of a great estate only developed by this singular woman from a comparatively modern date.

Across the driveway stands a 30 feet high bank of the large-leaved *Rhododendron macabeanum. R edgeworthii,* tinged pink and strongly scented, enjoys the shelter of its larger companions. A towering hybrid of *R. arboreum* has reached 40 feet. Conifers here include the stately *Pinus radiata, Sequoia sempervirens* and several wellingtonias, *Sequoiadendron giganteum.*

Along the path leading round the lake the largest *Eucalyptus regnans* in the British Isles has reached approximately 80 feet since it was planted in the early 1950's.

Here also is a good specimen of a felted, glaucous-leaved *Rhododendron eriogynum* hybrid carrying red flowers in June. Close to the pathway, the imposing *Weinmannia trichosperma* is seen in only a very few gardens. This mainly tropical genus has only two relatively hardy species in Britain providing white flowers and very attractive pinnate leaves. Here too is found the best *Sophora tetraptera* in the garden. Rhododendrons too are scattered or growing in clumps around the trees on this side of the lake. They include the poppy red *R. griersonianum* and *R. diaprepes*, useful in producing its white flowers very late.

Splendid cross views of the lake side from either bank are a strong feature. The lake itself is artificial, created by the 3rd Marquess in 1846-48. Its banks have been planted with the giant-leaved *Gunnera manicata*, royal ferns, arums, sedges, willows and poplars.

Towards the end of the lake, an area culminating in the wall and corner pavilions of Tir Na n-Óg, built as a private family burial ground, contains many rare and unusual plants, some tender. *Pseudopanax crassifolius* presents a striking appearance, a bare pole like stem with a mop of sword-like brown leaves at the top. *Cupressus cashmeriana* is by contrast perhaps the most graceful conifer, but unfortunately rather tender. *Cornus capitata* is again outstanding, but demands a mild climate.

On the wall of Tir Na n-Óg *Vallea stipularis* is still young but growing freely. The New Zealand *Metrosideros lucida* is only found in two other gardens in Ireland. The *Colquhounia coccinea* may be more familiar to visitors, although this very decorative Himalayan shrub bearing scarlet tubular flowers in late summer is not common and requires wall protection in almost all areas. Also to be included in the less than hardy category, the Australasian *Prostanthera rotundifolia* has tiny rounded leaves and carries a mass of lilac blue flowers in spring.

The surrounding area is also populated with many plants of distinction. Here can be seen *Hypericum leschenaultii*, a parent of the renowned *H*. "Rowallane", but rather more tender being a native of Java. In close proximity can be seen the interesting *Hydrangea aspera* with long narrow leaves quite different from the more frequently grown *H. aspera* var. *macrophylla,* which has large mounded foliage and flowers much more readily than the type.

Two other plants of distinction demand a mention. *Notelaea excelsa,* now known as *Picconia excelsa,* is related to the olives. The large bush here produces fragrant white flowers in late summer. The real olive, *Olea europaea,* raised from seed collected in Jerusalem, does not seem to exactly relish its conditions but is now showing encouraging new bottom growth.

One of the later garden developments was the Jubilee Glade stretching eastward at the head of the lake. This was planted in 1935 to commemorate the silver Jubilee of King George V and Queen Mary. The original colour scheme embraced the British national colours of red, white and blue. This area is now noteworthy for its autumn colour.

The path back along the other shore of the lake is known as The Ladies Walk along which the ladies of the house used to walk to the distant walled garden. It passes through a woodland area of great natural beauty aided by additional plantings of rhododendrons. These include a huge *R. decorum* of 25 feet, *R. griersonianum* and some of its splendid hybrids.

Where the woodland gives way to a glade the aristocrats of the rhododendron world display their charms: *R. sinogrande, R. falconeri, R. fictolacteum, R. hodgsonii* and *R. calophytum* are all here, still young plants but displaying very rapid growth and flowering well. The earlier flowering plants are followed by those dazzling reds *R. elliottii* and *R. eriogyum.*

Emerging at the north front of the house there can be seen directly facing the entrance a giant *Sequoiadendron* which stood at 114 feet when measured by Alan Mitchell in 1974. Three commemorative trees create an historical interest in this area. Two *Fagus sylvatica* forma *purpurea* were planted in 1903 on the occasion of a visit to Mount Stewart by King Edward VII and Queen Alexandra. A more recent planting was that of a *Metasequoia glyptostroboides* in 1952 by the Queen Mother.

Today this great garden is being maintained by the National Trust in a manner of which its inspired creator the late Lady Londonderry would undoubtedly approve. How fortunate that in the hands of the National Trust the future of this topmost garden is safeguarded for perpetuity.

Rowallane

County Down

Rowallane, Saintfield, Co Down
Telephone: (08) 0238 / 510131

From Belfast go south for 11 miles (20 Km) to Saintfield.
Follow signposts for Rowallane.

Visitors entering Rowallane in the spring season cannot but be impressed by the sheets of vivid red of the lofty tree rhododendrons, *R. arboreum*. These together with the unusual cairns of smooth stones along the driveway stand as a monument to the Rev. John Moore (1860-1903) the founder of this great 52 acre garden. His successor as owner was his nephew, Hugh Armytage Moore, a name revered in Irish horticulture, who in 1942 was awarded the Victoria Medal of Honour by the R.H.S. It is thought that much of the planting of the arboretum behind the house in the old pleasure ground area was part of his contribution to the great traditions of Rowallane. The older trees here can be attributed to his uncle who laid out this pleasure ground, and the younger ones have been added by the National Trust. In 1955 the gardens passed into the hands of the National Trust who today have established it as their headquarters with the lovely nineteenth century mansion serving as administrative offices and a conference centre. No more fitting location could be found than mid-Down, a county that contains all three of Northern Ireland's great open gardens.

The drive approach is studded with much fine timber and some magnificent specimen rhododendrons. The most outstanding tree here is *Chamaecyparis lawsoniana* "Kilmacurragh", which measures 42 feet and is the tallest of its kind recorded in the British Isles. In front of the house banks of rhododendrons, some of massive proportions, fill the view, with a large *Lomatia ferruginea* near the driveway taking over the stage in later summer. The fact that this thrives in full exposure reveals the very favourable climatic aspect of this garden.

The walled garden to the left of the house contains a nice mixture of herbaceous plants and tender shrubs. A very comprehensive collection of *Meconopsis* is scattered along the northern borders; these include *M. grandiflora* with narrow lanceolate leaves and wide blue saucer flowers, and *M. quintuplinerva* from China with flowers of mid-purple. Early in the summer, the large yellow flowered *Rhododendron* "Crest" shows a touch of class. Of the herbaceous plants, the rose coloured *Bergenia* "Ballawley" is also flowering, as is *Pulmonaria officinalis*, an old but seldom seen member of the lungwort family. Later in the summer a large bush of *Hoheria lyallii* delights with its drape of fragrant white blossom. Around the same time the herbaceous *Clematis recta* bears its dainty white racemes of flowers. A special feature of this garden is the rose coloured primula of its own raising known as *P.* "Rowallane Rose". Also preserved here is the baneberry *Actaea spicata*, a local plant of the Northern English limestones, but absent from Ireland. This shrubby member of the buttercup family produces racemes of white flowers in May. In the range of dwarf shrubs, a three-foot-high willow, *Salix helvetica*, mid-European in origin, gives a pleasing effect with small catkins that appear with the leaves. Another of the garden's own plants is *Viburnum plicatum* "Rowallane", a small grower which carries decorative fruits in autumn. To the left of the gateway leading out of this garden is a conifer difficult to recognise as such. This is the celery pine, *Phyllocladus alpinus*, carrying purple flower heads in late May.

Passing into the outer walled garden complete with lily pond, an uncommon white *Paeonia wittmanniana* stands out in the border, which also contains the Australian shrub *Acradenia frankliniae* with clusters of white flowers in May. This section has the special attraction of another Rowallane plant, the *Chaenomeles* X *superba* "Rowallane", whose blood-red colour cannot but excite. Nothing, however, can rival the allurement of the white *Rhododendron* "Lady Alice Fitzwilliam", just beside the archway. Its compelling vanilla scent fills the air while its long trumpet flowers are pure perfection. In the Haggard Paddock outside, formerly a farm stackyard, the stately *Populus maximowiczii* covers the grass lawn with its hundreds of fallen lamb's wool catkins.

More rhododendrons screened by an outer shelter belt are the main feature of that area known as the Spring Ground; it does, however, also contain that colourful autumn subject *Oxydendrum arboreum*. The colouring could be compared to that of *Parrotia* but it is not so easy to grow and requires an acid soil.

Adjoining this is the rock garden which is no ordinary rockery but one on the grand scale, where a hill of rock outcrop has been unobtrusively tailored to suit planting requirements. The tree heaths *Erica arborea*, with fragrant white flowers, are the only tall growing shrubs used on the summit, but at other levels occasional tall growing shrubs such as *Stranvaesia* have been introduced. The primulas which form the main late spring display, after the early flowering heathers have faded, are planted in prepared pockets in clumps of one variety. Again *P.* "Rowallane Rose" gains a favoured position in a rock enclave. Some dwarf rhododendrons also feature, which include the unusual *R. trichostomum*, an aromatic white or rose coloured species with tiny leaves. *R. hanceanum*, covered in lemon-yellow minature flowers, is another enchanting dwarf. But probably more widespread acclaim will be aroused by the many evergreen Japanese azaleas in shades ranging from pink to vivid carmine, and the autumn interest is maintained with the late flowering *Erica* and *Calluna*.

The adjoining Old Wood succeeds very well in showing off its collection of rhododendrons in a natural setting of open woodland, the timber being mostly beech and that formerly indigenous conifer, the Scots pine, so attractive in its bark colour and cleanness of stem. The light shade provided here accentuates the colour of that splendid geranium-red *Rhododendron* "May Day", much more freely flowering than its famous parent. Close to the wall may be seen the darkest coloured of the rhododendrons, *R. sanguineum* ssp. *didymum*, whose small bell shaped flowers are a dark black plum colour. This shady glade provides an ideal setting for the rather tender red tree heath *Erica australis*.

Away to the right can be seen the largest mound of *Desfontainia spinosa* to be found in any Irish garden. This is an alluring plant with its small holly-like leaves and narrow orange-red tubular flowers, but unfortunately is not altogether hardy and liable to disappoint in colder areas. It is interesting to observe that in this seemingly very sheltered garden new shelter belts are still being planted at points on the perimeter.

The next section of the garden, called The Paddock, houses the most comprehensive collection of shrubs from the Rosaceae family, including *Prunus, Sorbus* and *Crataegus,* assembled in any garden. Many old favourites are on view but also some very interesting newer introductions. There are also some other good items here, including two splendid acers. From central China comes *A. maximowiczii,* of modest size but very distinctive in its rose tinted foliage which deepens in shade as the season advances. The other which caught my attention was *A. palmatum* var. *heptalobum.* This Japanese maple has rather large leaves with dark crimson tinting. Of the *Sorbus* collection *S. vilmorinii* is attractive because it is perfectly suited to the smaller garden and has attractive fern-like leaves which turn a brilliant red in autumn. The fruit clusters are a delicate rose red. *S. folgneri,* another medium-sized bush, has oval-toothed leaves which again produce rich autumn tints. Nor will *S. prattii,* with pearly white fruits, look outsize in any garden. The variety here is *subarachnoides,* whose leaves have an unusual cobwebby indumentum. *Malus hupehensis* provides soft pink fragrant flowers in spring and an even better autumn display of yellow fruit with delicate pink tints.

Another interesting tree here is the Washington thorn, *Crataegus phaenopyrum* with maple-like leaves and following the autumn tinting, a load of dark crimson berries. The tender evergreen Himalayan *Euonymus,* here labelled *pendulus* but better known as *lucidus,* has distinctive crimson young growth in spring. The birches look as elegant as ever in this elite company with *Betula lenta* showing its lovely bark coloured of deep mahogany, and *B. medwediewii* giving an autumn display with its huge golden leaves. Here in this garden is a member of the chestnut family worthy of mention. *Aesculus parviflora* coming from south-east America only reaches seven feet in height but has very long panicles of white flowers with red anthers.

Behind the house and walled garden lies a large parkland area dotted with a very interesting collection of conifers. Their presence lends a balance to this garden which in other areas has limited conifer representation. Here can be seen a mixture of some very young trees and those whose planting dates must correspond to the earliest development of the estate.

Among the more interesting specimens contained in this old Pleasure Ground is the big coned *Tsuga mertensiana* distinguished from the rest of hemlocks by the spread of its leaves all around the shoot. This tree, although growing in the wild in the most inhospitable sites, has not proved very free growing on good soils here. The tall, elegant shaped *Chamaecyparis lawsoniana* "Intertexta" carries a slight resemblance to *Cedrus deodara*. The rarest of the trees here with a very limited planting in Ireland is the deciduous *Glyptostrobus lineatus*. The leaves are similar to those of its relation *Taxodium* and are a rich brown in autumn.

Further Information

Many people who visit gardens and read books about them may for various reasons require additional information about gardens and the plants they contain. Such details are beyond the scope of this book, but this section suggests sources of further information.

Books

A visit to any bookshop or good library will reveal the wealth of books available about gardens and cultivated plants. However there are few books which deal with gardens and horticulture in Ireland. Some of the more generally useful include the following:

Irish Gardening and Horticulture edited by E. C. Nelson and A. Brady gives some historical and contemporary details of Irish horticulture.

Trees and Shrubs Cultivated in Ireland by M. Forrest gives a list of woody plants grown in most, but by no means all, of the larger Irish gardens and arboreta. A revised edition is being prepared at the time of writing.

The Gardens of Ireland by M. George and P. Bowe describes and illustrates a number of Irish gardens, many of which are, however, not normally open to the public.

Some of the gardens mentioned in the text have produced leaflets or booklets which describe the gardens and their plants.

There are many books which deal specifically with the description or cultivation of garden plants. Many are highly detailed accounts of special groups such as rhododendrons, conifers and others. The following texts are more general in scope:

Trees and Shrubs Hardy in the British Isles by W. J. Bean, now in its eighth edition and currently available in four volumes, with a supplement (by D. L. Clarke) published in 1988. These volumes provide a great deal of descriptive and horticultural information on hardy woody plants.

Dictionary of Gardening, also in four volumes, edited by F. J. Chittenden. Published for the Royal Horticultural Society, this work contains a wealth of information about all manner of cultivated plants and their cultivation. The nomenclature is now sadly out of date, despite a supplement edited by P. M. Synge, the second edition of which was published in 1969.

The European Garden Flora edited by S. M. Walters and others, of which three volumes of a projected six have so far been published. When completed, this will be a means of identification for almost all cultivated plants in Europe. Keys and descriptions are provided, but other information is of necessity very brief.

Societies

Anyone with a serious interest in gardens and horticulture would benefit from joining one of the many horticultural societies. Some of the larger national organisations are listed below, with contact addresses. These societies hold regular meetings and lectures, publish periodicals and organise a variety of events.

The Irish Garden Plant Society, c/o The National Botanic Gardens, Glasnevin, Dublin 9.

The Royal Horticultural Society of Ireland, Swanbrook House, Bloomfield Avenue, Morehampton Road, Donnybrook, Dublin 4.

The Heritage Gardens Committee, a sub-committee of An Taisce, Taylor's Hall, Back Lane, Dublin 8.

There are many specialist societies which deal with particular groups of plants, such as pelargonium, rhododendrons, alpines, roses and others. The majority of them are British-based, but have local groups active in both Northern Ireland and the Irish Republic. Finally, there are a great number of local horticultural societies, many of which organise outings, exchange plants and invite speakers to address their meetings. A useful, but by no means complete list of addresses can be found in *Irish Gardening News, Yearbook 1990*.

Index of Gardens

Botanical Index

Plants are listed by their scientific names. Synonyms and common names
are only given where they are mentioned in the text.

ABELIA
    X *grandiflora*   206
ABIES (Firs)
    alba (Silver Fir)   145,156
    bornmuelleriana   28
    bracteata   89
    cephalonica   28
    concolor var. *Iowania*   158
    delavayi var. *faxoniana*   30,197
    delavayi var. *forrestii*   120,130
    delavayi var. *georgei*   130,198
    firma   187
    fraseri   197
    grandis   186
    koreana   6
    lasiocarpa (Alpine Fir)   143
    magnifica   14
    nordmanniana (Caucasian Fir)   28,95,158,188,206
    pinsapo (Spanish Fir)   89
    procera (Noble Fir)   6
    procera "Glauca"   150
    procera "Nana"   6
    spectabilis   79
ABUTILON
    "Ashford Red"   38
ACACIA (Wattles)
    baileyana   38
    melanoxylon   71,96
    pravissima   80
    riceana   204
ACER (Maples)   7,105,110,111,156,158
    cappadocicum   132
    ginnala   7,132
    griseum   132,187
    grosseri var. *hersii*   180
    maximowiczii   216
    nikoense   55,132
    oliverianum   132
    palmatum var. *heptalobum* "Osakazuki"   102,111,216

231

NANDINA
    domestica (Sacred Bamboo)   38,112
NARCISSUS sp. (Daffodils)   5,125
NEOLITSEA
    sericea   69
NERINE sp.   54
NESOCODON
    mauritianus   88
NOTHOFAGUS (Southern Beeches)   158
    dombeyi (Chilean Beech)   33,179,197
    moorei   173
    procera   197
NYSSA
    sylvatica (Tupelo Tree)   89,180
ODONTIODA
    "Drumbeat"   72
OLEA
    europaea (Olive)   209
OMPHALODES
    cappadocica (Blue Eyed Mary)   126
OTANTHUS (Cottonweed)
    maritimus   87
OSMUNDA
    regalis (Royal Fern)   47,208
OXYDENDRUM
    arboreum   215
PAEONIA (Peony)   7
    delavayi   127
    lutea   127
    wittmanniana   214
    "Anne Rosse"   127
PARROTIA
    persica   6,69,89,96,120,164,215
PARROTIOPSIS
    jaquemontiana   89
PASSIFLORA (Passion Flower)   113
    caerulea   29
    quadrangularis   88
PAULOWNIA
    tomentosa   205
PELARGONIUM sp.   88
PELTIPHYLLUM
    peltatum (Umbrella Plant)   17
PHORMIUM
    tenax   187

Pinus (cont.)
pinea "Fragilis"	71
radiata (Monterey Pine)	95,118,207
sylvestris (Scots Pine)	55,103,110,111,119,151,215
sylvestris var. *aurea*	196,197
tabuliformis	156
torreyana	188

PIPTANTHUS
laburnifolius	38

PITTOSPORUM
eugenioides	205
tenuifolium "Garnettii"	41,104

PLAGIANTHUS
betulinus	86

PLATANUS (Planes)
acerifolia	132

PODOCARPUS
andinus	22,78,144
dacrydioides	198
macrophyllus "Aureus"	78
salignus	17,173,178
totara	17

POLYSTICHUM | 158
setiferum	128

PONCIRUS
trifoliata (Bitter Orange)	127

POPULUS (Poplars) | 166,208
canescens	130
lasiocarpa	128
maximowiczii	215

POTENTILLA sp. | 89

PRIMULA
florindae	17
Candelabra types	22,57
"Rowallane Rose"	214,215

PROSTANTHERA
rotundifolia	208

PRUNUS (Cherries, Plums) | 62,144,187,216
laurocerasus (Common Laurel)	206,207
laurocerasus "Camelliifolia"	104
sargentii	129
serrula	86
subhirtella	129
"Accolade"	129

PSEUDOLARIX
amabilis (Golden Larch)	40,188

Rhodendron (cont.)

ciliatum	33
cinnabarinum	7,40,47
cinnabarinum var. *blandfordiiflorum*	16
cinnabarinum var. *roylei*	7
crassum	31,207
crinigerum	62
dalhousiae	56,63
decorum	62,209
delavayi	16
detonsum	72
diaprepes	208
edgeworthii	95,207
elliottii	209
eriogynum	32,208,209
falconeri	16,31,47,56,63,94,207,209
fictolacteum	209
fortunei	54
fulgens	64
genesterianum	54
griersonianum	32,47,56,63,64,118,208,209
griffithianum	63
haematodes	40,64
hanceanum	215
henryi	158
hodgsonii	209
impeditum	41
insigne	63
keiskei	97
lepidostylum	33
leucapsis	54
lindleyi	48
lutescens	49
macabeanum	31,48,207
mallotum	64
megacalyx	48
mollyanum	48
moupienense	54
neriiflorum	63
nuttallii	63
orbiculare	95
ponticum	61
ponticum "Cheiranthifolium"	72
praestans	63
racemosum	40

Rhodendron (cont.)

recurvoides	62
rex	9
sanguineum ssp. *didymum*	215
sinogrande	56,94,209
sperabile	63
taggianum	39
thompsonii	63,96
trichostomum	215
ungernii	145
wardii	16,54,199
williamsianum	95
xanthocodon	63
yakushimanum	6,40,145
yunnanense	63,205
zeylanicum	97
Azalea types	7,22,49,120,164,215
Kurume Azalea	78
"Amaura"	32
"Amoena"	105
"Ascot Brilliant"	63
"Augfast"	33
"Avalanche"	64,97
"Blue Diamond"	16,63
"Blue Tit"	16,63
"Bric-a-Bric"	54
"Cornish Cross"	63
"Cornubia"	16
"Crest"	199,214
"Dairymaid"	63
"Fabia"	47
"Frangrantissimum"	95
"Grierdal"	56
"Lady Alice Fitzwilliam"	39,48,54,214
"Lady Chamberlain"	64
"Lady Rosebery"	40
"Loderi"	64,96
"Loderi King George"	97
"May Day"	64,215
"Penjerrick"	32
"Prelude"	54
"Princess Alice"	39,48
"Seta"	80,145
"Shilsonii"	16,96
"Tally Ho"	32,47,63

Women Surviving
Studies in the History of Irish Women in the 19th and 20th centuries

Edited by

Maria Luddy and Cliona Murphy

This highly original collection of historical articles addresses aspects of women's history in nineteenth and early twentieth-century Ireland, including: nuns in society; paupers and prostitutes; the impact of international feminists on the Irish suffrage movement and women's contribution to post-Independence Irish politics.

POOLBEG

A Strange Kind of Loving

by Sheila Mooney

A touching, searingly honest and at times heartbreaking account of an upbringing in an Ascendancy family and the author's vain attempts to win the love and approval of her Victorian father while continuing to support her beautiful, eccentric and alcoholic mother. Sheila Mooney is the sister of 1930s Hollywood idol, Maureen O'Sullivan, and her memoir contains witty and illuminating accounts of her career.

POOLBEG